ENERGY
BLESSINGS
from the
STARS

SEVEN INITIATIONS

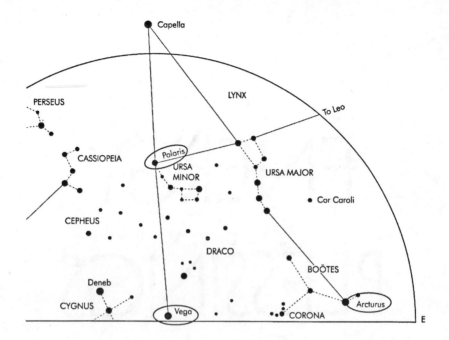

Star map for a portion of the No. Hemisphere in February.
Look for Arcturus, Polaris, & Vega.

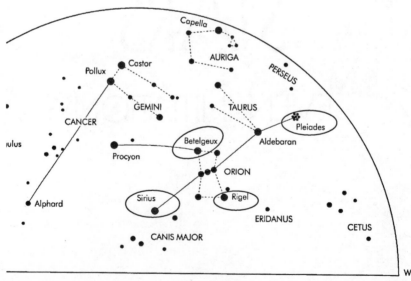

Star map for a portion of the No. Hemisphere in February.
Look for Pleiades, Betelgeuse (Betelgeux), Rigel, & Sirius.

ENERGY
BLESSINGS
from the
STARS
SEVEN INITIATIONS

VIRGINIA ESSENE
& IRVING FEURST

 S.E.E. Publishing Company, Santa Clara, California, USA

This book is manufactured in the United States of America.
Printed on recycled paper.

Cover Design: Lightbourne Images

ISBN # 0-937147-29-X
Library of Congress Catalog Card Number: 98-061252

Spiritual Education Endeavors
Publishing Company
1556 Halford Avenue, #288
Santa Clara, CA 95051-2661 USA
Tel. (408) 245-5457

VIRGINIA'S DEDICATION

I dedicate this book to our Mother/Father Creator...to the wise and loving guides of all dimensions, times, and places who patiently help us remember and express our Divine Consciousness...and to all life forms everywhere who positively contribute to the preservation of life and the expression of love, compassion and wisdom.

It is a special joy to honor all of my awakened sisters and brothers who strive for peace, and who protect our exquisite planet and her many wondrous kingdoms and species.

Virginia Essene

IRVING'S DEDICATION

May we all come to know our innermost God nature and be able to express it outwardly in our life. And may this book be of help in that process.

Irving Feurst

VIRGINIA'S ACKNOWLEDGMENTS

This book has received the support of a dedicated band of helpers, some involved with the Share Foundation/S.E.E. Publishing Company for many years. Special bouquets go to: Alma Scheer, our office manager, for her consistent devotion and invaluable assistance in innumerable ways...to Pat Proud, for her esteemed editorial support in this eighth book publication...to Ron Cantoni for his greatly valued desktop publishing and editorial service...to Jan Ricksecker for her encouragement and manuscript aid...to our bookkeeper Ravelle McRhoads for all her help...to John Afton, our remarkable legal resource and friend in spirit...and to my dedicated spiritual brother, Irving Feurst, who fulfilled his soul promise to complete this meritorious project, a task he never sought and which required considerable personal sacrifice.

I also wish to acknowledge all past financial contributors to the Share Foundation's work including a recent love donation from Holly Joy/Immanuel Johnson-Merano whose contribution has assisted in the publication of this particular volume.

IRVING'S ACKNOWLEDGMENTS

Many people have contributed to making the publication of this book a reality. Although this page is not big enough to list all of you by name, I want to acknowledge each and every one of you. Included are all of those who received the initiations and gave me feedback, all of those who read the manuscript and made suggestions, all of those who were involved in projects which were delayed while I worked on the book, Kristin Hemme for her word processing, Sherry Mouser for the interior illustrations*, Margo Shimasaki for transcribing many of the taped conversations between Virginia and myself, and of course Virginia herself for her love, vision and tireless dedication. Last, but certainly not least, I want to thank my wife, Judy, and son, Stefan, for their patience while I worked on a project which meant many lost hours of family time.

* Sherry Mouser can be contacted at smouser@pacbell.net

READER'S NOTES

We hope you will feel included by much of our book's deliberately conversational style from which many of the important aspects of the contents developed. There were many other questions that time and space did not allow us to include, as you might imagine. However, we trust that our inquiry will help you develop and meditate upon your own questions as you continue to resonate with the initiation energies offered in this book.

Because the Ascended Masters discussed within these pages do not require physical bodies or space vehicles for transportation or communication, it was our joint decision to use the term "non-terrestrial" when referring to them, rather than extra-terrestrial, alien, or other terms which could possibly suggest physical rather than spiritual beings.

Irving and Virginia are frequently asked to suggest an appropriate meditation style for individuals who are just beginning the meditation process. While we both agree that meditation is best learned from a living teacher, a book entitled How to Meditate by Lawrence LeShan is recommended for those presently unable to acquire a physical teacher.

The primary sources for our astronomical data are StarList 2000 by Richard Dibon-Smith and Burnham's Celestial Handbook by Robert Burnham, Jr.—two standard and highly recommended resources. The star maps, with annotations, are from The Observer's Year by Patrick Moore.

CONTENTS

Chapter 1   *Virginia's Welcome and Introduction* 1

Chapter 2   *Irving's Personal Story* 15

Chapter 3   *Energy* 41

Chapter 4   *Initiation* 61

Chapter 5   *Arcturus – the Blessing of Hope* 81

Chapter 6   *Polaris – the Blessing of Breath* 95

Chapter 7   *Pleiades – the Blessing of Love* 109

Chapter 8   *Vega – the Blessing of Compassion* 129

Chapter 9   *Betelgeuse – the Blessing of Expanded Soul Awareness* 149

Chapter 10   *Rigel – the Blessing of the Integration of Matter with Spirit* 169

Chapter 11   *Sirius – the Blessing of Amplified and Glorified Christ Consciousness* 189

Chapter 12   *New Hope for Humanity* 209

Appendix A   *The Seven Rays of Creation* A-1

Appendix B   *Solar Angel Contract* B-1

Appendix C   *Keeping an Initiation Diary* C-1

Chapter I

VIRGINIA'S WELCOME AND INTRODUCTION

If you felt drawn to read the material in Energy Blessings from the Stars, you are probably a seeker of truth. As a seeker you will certainly have considered many universal questions about the meaning of life. It is the purpose of this book to honor your inquiry and to help deepen your ability to ponder the vastness of creation, its unspeakably awesome activities, and your own role in fulfilling the expanding consciousness on planet Earth. For the Earth is not separate from the purpose and activities of the universe in which we dwell, and spiritual guidance energies are all around us! I believe we have access to these very powerful spiritual energies at every moment and that assistance can come from wonderful teachers and helpers, both on Earth and in higher dimensions. In this book we will focus on the non-terrestrial Ascended Masters presently willing to empower our own sincere efforts to grow and serve life.

For those who desire spiritual guidance, this book is an energy portal for receiving transformative energy initiations directly from spiritual masters in seven different star systems. There are many such masters at work independently, but this is a Cosmic Consortium plan by a group who have deliberated and designated the seven most necessary energy qualities they believe human beings need at this moment in their evolution. To increase these particular qualities in us they now offer them—through the process called initiation—to those humans ready and willing to participate.

These are the stars from which the masters are ready to send their energy blessings:

ARCTURUS...offers you the blessing of *Hope* through which all things become possible

POLARIS...offers you the blessing of *Breath* to help release past limitations

PLEIADES...offers you the blessing of *Love* to safely open your heart chakra

VEGA...offers you the blessing of *Compassion* to use for yourself and others

BETELGEUSE...offers you the blessing of expanded *Soul Awareness*

RIGEL...offers you the blessing of wholeness from the *Integration of Matter with Spirit*

SIRIUS...offers you the blessing of amplified and glorified *Christ Consciousness*

As many of us on Earth, through our small steps into space, become more aware of the galaxy's awesome magnitude, we may find ourselves asking, "Who are we? Why are we here? And what is this mysterious divine plan which seems to tug at our heart strings to remember and express?"

So much of it seems unknowable. Despite our scientific explorations and our wonderful advancements in space, who among us understands the mysterious cycles and rhythms of all the celestial realms?

In order to have even the simplest perception of how it is possible for us to receive energy blessings from the stars, we humans must expand our limited concepts concerning Earth's minuscule physical location within a rather ordinary-sized galaxy called the Milky Way. Since our galaxy is but one of many millions of such formations in the universe, this knowledge should immediately cause us a deep feeling of humility about our value and identity in that unspeakably vast cosmic expression. Please refer to the illustration to observe our Sun's

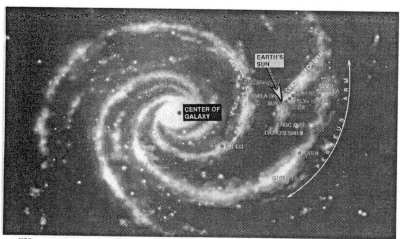

Illustration showing the Milky Way Galaxy and our Sun.

location in the galaxy (see above).

When you note that our Sun and its small family of planets—our solar system—is about 30,000 light-years away from the major center of galactic activity designated as the "Central Sun," you may realize that we are quite removed from its incredible light and power. Just as we humans have suburbs, rural, and remote areas on our planet, so in similar fashion the Earth resides in the remote outskirts of the galaxy's boundaries. Out here, off of one of our galaxy's major spiraling arms, a smaller spur began its physical life by coagulating the gases and dusts and debris of creation to form new opportunities for existence. Uncountable planets and stars were created in this cauldron of experimentation where various biological processes of life developed long before our particular Sun, and its various solar system companions, began to function. Therefore, we must realize that although we have not seen all of these physical places around our Earth's creation, except by their astronomical fingerprints, there have been a myriad of unique life forms birthed before us. In some of these matter worlds, certain life forms managed to evolve sufficiently so that their species were identified by nearby spiritual mentors as being ready for the "ensouling" process. This soul

3

gift—or you could call it the gift of consciousness from God—was passed down in the correct frequency appropriate for the species' dimensional vibration. Because this cosmic womb of creation has so many dimensional levels of physical matter and spiritual consciousness, it is only through the auspices of trusted spiritual emissaries in various of the far flung regions that a watchful eye is maintained to determine if the ensoulment gift should be granted. Only when a life form has been identified as "ready for consciousness" do the emissaries of light report this readiness and the powerful gift of God's nature—a soul—is energized or initiated into them. Cosmic history is surely replete with examples of life beyond our imagining, as we have seen in our science fiction books and films of recent years. Some of us retain these deep unconscious memories which assist us in achieving greater clarity during certain celestial cycles often called the precession of the equinoxes. Whatever these energies are, they are cyclic portals or dimensional windows during which God's celestial rays and the spiritual mentors are enormously empowered. Thus the rays and our spiritual connections oversee humanity's evolutionary process and bring forth higher energies to support and stimulate our consciousness. When scientists and creationists can explore these challenging concepts with open minds and hearts, and join in understanding that humanity is both a physical and a spiritual being, certain cooperative ventures to make humanity's advancement more joyfully profound will be possible.

A major question to ponder is whether mere biological evolution—left only to its own impulses—can create the higher spiritual consciousness of a soul through its own power—or whether a higher presence of celestial consciousness must be involved in determining when a life form may be ready to receive this gift of consciousness since matter is a lower organizational level. Obviously, the secrets of the universe cannot be given to a novice who is not capable of understanding the responsibilities that the gift of soul consciousness requires. Particularly when, in the lower dimensional frequencies, God's gift of free will can be so powerfully misused during the early stages of consciousness! Would you grant the supernatural powers that higher initiations could bring to a free will person until you had ascertained that compassion and love were permanent aspects of their behavior? As an adult person would you grant a young child the power of thought control over other people before they were wise enough to be trusted with it? Probably not.

We of the technological societies have a tendency to think we can behave however we want because we feel alone on Earth and free to do as we please, regardless of whom it affects. Because so many remnants of negative Atlantean and Roman experiences remain in the consciousness of citizens in the major technological nations, we find any suggestion of being controlled—even when change is for the best interest of the planet, other people, and other living things—to be distasteful. So there needs to be a plan to aid humanity that assists it but requires integrity and moral responsibility in return. I believe that if you were a spiritual mentor desiring to help human beings advance into higher states of consciousness, you might well attempt to offer an upgrade in consciousness to that entire species, provided that the gift couldn't backfire and be harmful to others.

As you continue reading this book you will be made aware that such a plan has been initiated by the higher realms and that you can accept that gift, provided you are willing to do two required things to be explained later in greater detail. We humans have been ensouled. We have free will. The rest of the story is up to each one of us personally.

I believe we are children of the stars who have a divine heritage to remember and claim for ourselves, for our children and for posterity. The energy blessings are all around us, and for those who are willing to learn and grow, these energy blessings merely await our awareness and request. Every known religion has promised blessings such as grace, forgiveness, wisdom and love to all who would willingly cooperate with the divine plan. They give us guidance and teachings, and yet throughout recent history humanity falls short. Are we finally ready to accept the gifts promised our prodigal species from the very beginning?

Imagine for a moment that, in a long ago Earthean civilization, you once had enormous energy initiations from beings of higher wisdom and caring—from those spiritual ones who were guides for this particular planet's advancement into higher dimensions. Imagine that as these masters identified specific humans who were pure of heart and mind, they began to initiate, teach, and guide them. Groups were formed and various qualities were actually transmitted to groups by some spiritual master's touch. This transference of heavenly energy filled with purity, wisdom and love, given by one who believed the recipient could be trusted not to misuse the power being shared, was an enormous gift. It was a high frequency energy that "jump-started" or awoke their own body's energy systems, increasing the kinds of dormant power their own minds and bodies possessed. Gradually, by their dedication to enlightenment, humans were trusted to receive these supernatural, fantastic powers.

They could levitate off the ground and bi-locate their bodies in different locales. They became fully clairvoyant, clairaudient, clairsentient, telepathic, and able to create material objects with their minds. By today's abilities, they were rather godlike in their co-creative power, and some of them began to experiment with controlling physical matter, life itself, through use of their mind's intention only.

Unfortunately, there were such flagrant abuses of these extraordinary powers that the masters questioned whether further spiritual initiations would be appropriate. Extreme misuse finally caused the spiritual guardians to withdraw those energy initiations that had previously been allowed. So we humans on planet Earth today, for the most part, are presently missing certain energy capabilities that some humans living here previously enjoyed. I believe that is why some of us are so frustrated by our current situation here on Earth. Where there can be cooperation, love and peace, we see violence and evil. Sometimes we ourselves fail to behave with the purity and caring that we know is needed.

Fortunately, we are living at a unique and momentous time. The prodigal species is being invited to a great banquet of blessings, and the promises of heavenly energy filled with wisdom, love and purity are deeper and richer than we can imagine.

We need to be mindful that the potential for these initiations requires effort and change on our part, and is not a handout, a UFO lift-off, or an excuse to ignore our inner work! Many of us, especially in technological and materialistic societies tend to be quite lazy and undisciplined about our spiritual responsibilities. However, it is time now to devote ourselves to this ongoing practice of attaining inner healing that earns the notice and support from our spiritual mentors. This is the first time they have offered energy initiations of this power for many, many years, patiently waiting for a shift in human consciousness that could be trusted. This shift will allow our continued journey toward achievement of the seven attributes of Christ Consciousness, which all or part of humanity can attain.

There's no need to feel guilty or upset when realizing that a prior "practice period" toward the achievement of Christhood was thwarted because of our own, and others, errors! Rather let us focus on the tools of love and forgiveness which many masters, saints, and sages bring to us in their models of purity and commitment. It serves us well to acknowledge that there is a divine plan for our beautiful Earth and her inhabitants that leads to Christhood, Buddhahood, or whatever term you wish. These great ones came to show us the way, to support our self-chosen growth, but not to rescue us from our egotistical weaknesses and unwillingness to change. Even if the masters wanted to wave away our follies and rescue us from ourselves, they could not. Therefore, we must each make choices about the level of our cooperation with their divine energies. But how many of us know what choices we really have to advance in consciousness and what areas of self-development are critical? As seekers of truth, are we fully aware that we have four choices of spiritual contact open to us at this particular time in human evolution to help us master existence? Do you feel confident that you know what they are and how they can assist human evolution?

It is my personal belief that wherever we live in physical bodies on the various planets throughout our galaxy and beyond, we make progress in our abilities to use energy and consciousness according to our positive free will choices. Whenever we've been in a physical body we have always had available the following three choices of interaction with the energies of enlightenment: Faith in something greater...acknowledging God's energy for daily living...and initiation through earthly physical contact. Choice, of course, means that a person could say yes or no. And as we'll learn, there is now a new and exciting fourth choice possible.

CHOICE NUMBER ONE:
FAITH IN SOMETHING GREATER

You may choose to understand—or to deny—that everything is energy and consciousness, and that these substances contain all of the Creator's, or God's, vast love and unspeakable wisdom. There are people on planet Earth who don't believe in anything beyond what they can see, and haven't even considered the possibility something grander exists. And they are allowed to keep this perception. What has your own choice been?

CHOICE NUMBER TWO:
ACKNOWLEDGING GOD'S ENERGY
FOR DAILY LIVING

You may choose to understand—or deny—that you are surrounded by the Creator's intelligent and loving energy on Earth, or wherever you go in the galaxy or universe(s). This energy will always respond to your prayers, your cry for help, regardless of what you call it or to whom you address your plea.

CHOICE NUMBER THREE:
INITIATION THROUGH EARTHLY PHYSICAL CONTACT

You may choose to understand—or deny—that since the beginning of life here on Earth, there have been many great physical beings of light who have taught and shared their truths with the evolving human consciousness. These masters of energy, sometimes called gurus, have created ongoing healing lineages that are present even today, through the power of their touch, look, or intent. Such a master's gift is given to open the correct circuitry in the initiate's body so that the life-giving flow of energy brings about the balance of the physicalness of Earth and the highest spiritual nature.

If there were enough gurus on the planet, if they remained forever true to their high spiritual calling, and if enough people took advantage of the valuable attunements they offer, then humanity would be much further along in spiritual consciousness. From the standpoint of the heavenly realms, there are far too few earthly gurus for the billions of humans needing to be uplifted as our planet Earth moves into her destiny of higher consciousness. Consequently her own expansion and advancement would be aided if more humans could simultaneously achieve similar positive growth to match her own. Having a spiritual initiation not only helps us as individuals, but it also aids the entire human family, the planet, and many other life forms. Also, it would increase the spiritual base upon which incoming babies could quickly become expressions of a more conscious civilization. Moreover, initiations containing wisdom, love, and compassion for a large number of people would quickly assure a higher vibrational world ready for another great spiritual/vibrational teacher or teachers, and a greater, faster, human evolution.

These three choices—faith in something greater, acknowledging God's energy for daily living, and initiation through earthly physical contact—are still available today. That has not changed. What has changed now is choice number four, the recent opportunity to receive cosmic initiations or blessings from the stars.

CHOICE NUMBER FOUR:
COSMIC INITIATIONS

You can choose to understand—or deny—that energy blessings from the stars are presently available to help you grow. Fortunately, in this auspicious and very exciting time, these energy blessings come to assist our spiritual aspirations and empower our endeavors to heal ourselves, and to do everything in our power to improve the moral fiber of earthly life. They come as another part of the cosmic dispensation which allows us to surrender fear, hatred, guilt, and other negative beliefs and emotions.

For those who choose this spiritual awakening, the seven energy blessings from the stars will infuse our subtle body energy fields with various sacred components of spiritual balance, eventually leading to Christ Consciousness. However, our readiness for these life-changing divine energies is dependent upon: *strengthening the subtle body energy fields so that higher perceptions can be realized...and raising their vibrational rate so that their energy patterns and structure are capable of holding the other available higher gifts.* This first initiation, a strengthening gift to the subtle body fields, is the essential foundation for all the remaining initiations to follow.

The second preparatory cosmic initiation is for *releasing the glamours of the illusionary world.* The choice to release all the glamours of the world can be nearly impossible in today's civilization. The term "anti-glamour initiation" refers not only to releasing obsession with physical beauty, but also spiritual self-righteousness, extreme nationalism and any other illusion of superiority that would separate us from each other. This includes every aspect of human life, in areas such as cultural, racial, sexual, religious, economic and political concerns, and just about anything else you can think of. When you accept this initiation, it will be active throughout the rest of your life.

The spiritual masters from the stars will know when you have sincerely requested these two preparatory initiations—and only after they have been requested and given can any of the other seven initiations be granted. In other words, you'll need the two preparatory energy cleansings and strengthening to "upgrade" your subtle body fields so they are capable of holding the higher energy gifts to follow. This plan of the Cosmic Consortium is carefully conceived to allow all humans these energy blessings provided they are sincerely willing to use this experience of cosmic healing for the highest good.

Perhaps you have been experiencing a variety of unusual, even disturbing energetic influences these days that you don't quite understand. Since we have no personal control over the cosmic rays and celestial energies that influence our planet and all of life, our only hope is to balance our own personal energy fields in such a way that we can effectively cooperate with these massive changes from a point of clarity. Those who have the awareness and inner resolution to be stimulated and transformed through this cosmic healing opportunity will be amplifying the Buddhic and Christed qualities that imbue spiritual truth in the physical reality. This is the role of every human being. The energy blessings from the stars will help us help ourselves if we choose to experience them.

This is not a casual "pie in the sky" experience. It is something practical for everyday living that has many challenges and even difficulties from time to time.

Have you ever felt uncomfortable living in your physical body and wished you were off in heaven somewhere? This is not an uncommon experience for those who are awakening and developing spiritually. It is, however, an experience that will distract you *from your true divine purpose, which is to master physical life using your spiritual resources.* The seven energy blessings offered from the stars will come to you while you are still in your physical body to help make life more joyful, creative and satisfying. They can aid in expansion of your daily expression as a responsible human on Earth and a celestial guardian of life.

As we enter the dawn of the 21st century together, it is vital to remember and express our true origins as humans who have three aspects demanding balance and expression.

We possess the eternal energy of universal consciousness. We possess the temporary form of our physical body—always remembering it is not separate from Mother Earth. We also possess thoughts/feelings, which either limit and imprison our true nature or release our wisdom and love for both personal and planetary healing. This trinity of beingness, which we seek to integrate with Mother Earth, allows us the power of co-creation in both individual and group consciousness decisions. It is therefore imperative for us to willingly provide the positive link of conscious thinking and feeling needed to express our divine pattern and purpose. Since the nature of existence is based on unified or holistic relationships and since any personal transformation is created by positive relationship, isn't an increasing positive relationship with nonterrestrial beings another release of our belief in separation?

You, of course, must discern your own path of belief and action, and proceed to accomplish your own heart and soul's desires. Hopefully, something contained within the pages of this book will inspire you, even aid you in accomplishing that celestial process. There are many comrades of light around the planet these days, and once we attune our energy and consciousness to similar purposes, wonderful synchronistic and synergistic connections can occur. Wonderful new friends appear, drawn by the similarity of consciousness and caring. Spiritual contacts become common, and love begins its natural and joyful flow.

I have had the honor of meeting so many people whose hearts and minds yearn for the return of divine principle to our earthly lives. But even if we do not meet in person, we are part of that vast resonating power that we can use in common agreement to manifest a better world for ourselves, our planet and life everywhere.

My co-author, Irving Feurst, is a comrade of light with whom I have been guided to write this book, and we both welcome you to a deeper inquiry into the use of consciousness and subtle life energies, and to the ever-expanding opportunities they presently allow.

Because Irving is a clairvoyant master of energy, I have asked him to share some of his life story with you before we proceed with the information on energy blessings from the stars. Then you can see, as I did, that Irving understands the many varieties of subtle energies and has the talent to explain more about them to the rest of us who are now ready to cooperatively apply them with high states of consciousness for constructive purposes.

May your perceptions be expanded by what you read here, and learn elsewhere, and may our common journey be enhanced by the visions we manifest, the loving companions we meet and treasure.

Chapter 2

IRVING'S PERSONAL STORY

Conversation between Virginia and Irving

VE (Virginia Essene): Irving, I'm sure your life story can really help us learn quite a lot about energy. Whatever prompted you to go into energy work?

IF (Irving Feurst): Well, for me, energy is a way to God. Energy is God in action. My spiritual path in this lifetime really started back in 1967, totally without my being aware of it. I was born and raised in Mississippi, and when I graduated from high school, I came to California to attend Stanford University as an undergraduate. At that time Stanford was experimenting with special seminars that freshmen could take on every conceivable subject in the world to make the freshman year more interesting. One of the courses was called "The Science of Creative Intelligence." Some people may recognize this as a phrase that the Transcendental Meditation movement used back then.

So I enrolled in this course because I was curious about meditation, was under a lot of stress, and heard meditation could help you relax. But, I had no interest in spirituality whatsoever. In fact, I was totally the opposite. I was very committed to a purely scientific, rational, atheistic worldview. I believed that the only thing that existed was matter and the laws of physics. There's a statement made by the Greek philosopher Lucretius thousands of years ago: "In reality, there are only atoms and the void." That's what I believed. I wanted to convince other people to accept this worldview. I was the village atheist type and I loved to argue with people about any metaphysical or spiritual beliefs and show them how wrong they were. And in all modesty, I was very good at it. In fact, one of my friends, who came from a long tradition of evangelistic atheists, said, "Irving, you've got arguments against the existence of God that even I have never heard before."

While taking this intellectually-oriented course, my roommate convinced me we should actually learn how to meditate so we went to the Transcendental Meditation Center in Berkeley to do just that. The person who initiated me was surprised by my ability to meditate and said, "Are you sure you've never meditated before?"

I meditated for many years after college, and I had a number of interesting experiences—none of which I would really label spiritual—more related to personal growth. If you want to put a label on them, I had Jungian type experiences, with archetypal images and energies. When I graduated from Stanford I went to graduate school at UC Berkeley, where I pursued degrees in both mathematics and statistics. At that time I began having spontaneous kundalini experiences even though I had no idea what kundalini was. I had never heard of it. All I knew was that while I was studying for my oral exams to earn my Master's degree, I had these bright white lights in the middle of my head, electrical feelings going up and down my spine, and I couldn't sleep at night.

What I eventually discovered was that the only way I could make these things go away was to stop meditating, which I did somewhat reluctantly because I enjoyed my meditation very much. But it was the only way I could get these disturbing experiences to stop.

For many years I taught and tutored math to a wide age range of students—from young children up to adults. My experience included teaching at the community college level as well as Project Seed, an organization which taught simple high school algebra to minority grade school children to improve their self-esteem.

Then about twelve years ago, I was in the middle of teaching a community college math class, when I noticed I had this awful pain in my neck. A lot of people wake up with a crick in the neck, from sleeping the wrong way on a pillow. But this pain didn't go away, and just kept getting worse and worse. I was finally forced to admit that I needed to see a doctor, who diagnosed me as having an unusual form of torticollis, a chronically stiff and painful neck. At this point my neck deteriorated so rapidly, I became bedridden for seven months. I very quickly became aware that traditional medicine didn't have any answers for me. My condition was considered a mystery problem. Nobody seemed to know what caused it or how to treat it. Very early on my wife found a Ph.D. thesis, which concluded that people who had pursued conventional medical techniques didn't show much improvement, or not nearly as much improvement as people who had pursued alternative methods. So, you name it, I did it. I could write an alternative healing book just on all the things that I did for my neck. I was selective in what I chose and I didn't do anything without some kind of evaluation, so everything that I did helped somewhat. However, the thing that helped me the most was working with energy.

When I say working with energy, I mean particularly working with shakti. That is the word that we use in the Spiritual Unfoldment Network (S.U.N.) to describe the energy that we use. (The evolution of the S.U.N., started by Irving, is discussed later in this chapter.) There really isn't a word in English to describe this kind of work. The word shakti is a Hindu term and some people in modern 20th century America use the word to simply mean energy. However, it's also used, as I use it, to refer to the concept of *intelligent spiritual energy*. That is to say, it's an energy that behaves intelligently.

I found that out of all the things that I tried, working with shakti helped the most. I still have torticollis. The energy work hasn't cured me totally, but it's what enables me to function. When I get up in the morning, I use certain energy techniques—particularly the Drisana energy and the Huna energy—and that's what enables me to get out of bed. If it weren't for this kind of energy work, I'd probably be spending many more hours a day in pain and incapacitated. So, it was because of my own personal health problems that I discovered energy work.

VE: Let me ask you, Irving, how did you learn to use shakti? How did you know that this energy existed and that you could use it on your behalf?

IF: Well, it wasn't something that happened overnight. It was an evolutionary process. Let me fill in some of the other steps here. When I became bedridden with this neck problem, I found that I was getting sucked into very deep meditative states, without my intending to. When I popped out of one I would look at the clock and find that four or five or six hours had gone by, and I was not even aware of time. I began having a recurrence of those spontaneous kundalini experiences, which I first had in the early seventies as a graduate student at Cal. For some reason I finally realized something that I hadn't realized in the seventies, which was that there was an intelligence behind these energies, and that I needed to let the process run to completion.

I began to go through a sequence of experiences (or steps) which to me are so eloquently described in classical Hinduism, where you begin to see everything in the universe as a manifestation of one underlying divine intelligence, which I would call God. I do believe in a personal God, although in our S.U.N. workshops we don't try to inflict any particular dogma on people. Some people prefer to think of Cosmic Mind or Source or Tao or whatever you want to call it. But I believe in a personal God, and I began experiencing everything in the universe as a manifestation of that God. However, I was extremely resistant to those experiences because I didn't want to give up the atheistic worldview, to which I was very wedded. So even though I was handed these profound experiences, I was doing everything I could to explain them away. It was actually a very tough time in my life. One of my most vivid memories from that period was sitting at the breakfast table one morning and seeing my teacup as God. And to tell you the truth, it scared the hell out of me because at that time I didn't believe in God, and I certainly didn't want to see God perched on my breakfast table in the form of this tea cup, spying on me, as it were.

These experiences were building up and becoming more and more powerful, and I was spending more and more hours every day trying to explain them away because they were getting so strong. They were very threatening to my ego. In the meantime, I tried acupuncture to help my neck. The treatments had an unexpected side effect of stimulating all kinds of spiritual experiences. The acupuncturist recommended I see Gurumayi. The first time I received shaktipat initiation from a human being in this lifetime was from Gurumayi, a woman guru, who is the head of a lineage called the Siddha lineage, which works with kundalini energy. I took an intensive from her, and when I entered that intensive I was still an atheist. On the first day, nothing much happened.

The second day was a very important day in my life, however, because I really experienced the shakti—like an electrical spark—going into my heart in a very profound way. There was a precise moment in time, which I can remember quite clearly, where my whole worldview changed. I shifted from being the village atheist to being someone who is spiritually oriented—who believes very strongly in the spiritual realm and the importance that it should play in our lives. It was a single instant in time where all the things that had been building up in me for years, and with increasing intensity in the few months prior to doing that intensive, crystallized. My resistance just went away. I realized that it is literally true that everything in the universe is a manifestation of one, underlying divine intelligence, which I would call God. This is not just a metaphor, or a delusion. I had tried to explain it away as a delusion but I now believe that even though we're meant to live in and enjoy the material world, it is not as important as the invisible, spiritual world, which underlies that, and from which the material world stems.

VE: So the guru really showed you evidence of intelligent energy and assisted your own personal energy experience.

IF: Yes, it was a very pivotal point in my life. After that intensive, as a result of the presence of that profoundly beautiful and very sweet shakti, which is the heritage of the Siddha lineage, I have felt the living presence of God every moment of my life. And that shakti has played a very important role in guiding me and in furthering my evolution. Since then I have experienced literally thousands of energies from many different cultures around the world, yet the Siddha shakti remains one of my favorite energies—not just for personal or historical reasons—but because the energy itself is so beautiful. That's one of the reasons why Gurumayi is so well known and has so many followers.

The next major step in my evolution occurred at a New Age fair. There was a booth by an organization called Omega. Now Omega teaches a very profound and very beautiful energy system, which came from the Tibetan master Djwhal Khul (hereafter referred to as D.K.), but at the time I really didn't have any knowledge of this. I was simply passing by this booth and felt this tremendous upsurge of the Siddha lineage shakti inside me. The shakti, which is a manifestation of God, advised, "Please go by that booth. Do that demonstration that they are offering." I said, "What?" And it said the same thing again. So I went over to that booth, and the people who were there demonstrated the Omega System for me. I didn't actually feel that much at the time, but I encouraged my wife to get a demonstration as well. Later that night we both had unusually strong experiences of seeing very vivid colors. I had experienced hypnogogic imagery many times before when I was going to sleep, yet this was in a class totally by itself. I had never experienced anything like it. So I called up the Omega organization and talked to them more about their system. As I was talking to them, the Siddha shakti came up again and suggested, "You should do this course."

Because it was a course being offered that weekend, I rearranged my affairs, and the Omega training got me further into energy work. I would say there were two main effects of working with Omega. The first thing it helped me realize is that there are many different energies. Omega was a different color, a different texture than the Siddha energy and it had different effects on me. My consciousness felt different when I was using it. At the time I didn't yet understand the concept that different energies come from different spiritual planes because I was focused primarily on the Siddha lineage shakti.

The second thing Omega energy introduced me to was the concept of a Spiritual Hierarchy. At first I was extremely resistant to this concept even though I believed in energy, and was having dramatic shifts almost daily in my ability to perceive and work with energy. I started seeing the world primarily as an exchange of energies, which totally changed my perception of how to be in the world. But I was very resistant to the concept of a Spiritual Hierarchy, or a group of what some people refer to as "Ascended Masters" who help guide the evolution of humanity. Omega really didn't push this concept in their literature but emphasized the energy itself and what it can do for people. We have the same approach in our Spiritual Unfoldment Network (S.U.N.). We want to attract people who are interested sincerely in furthering their own personal and spiritual evolution, not people who are attracted to the glamour of working with masters. As a result of taking Omega courses, I also learned about courses taught by the Christ Light Centers (CLC). From CLC courses I learned about the importance of the Solar Angel (what some call the guardian angel) and about an energy system called Lovestream.

Eventually I became aware from things the students said, and the incidental remarks that the Omega instructors made in class—that they believed the Omega energy came from this Spiritual Hierarchy. Well, I thought that this was a delusion, that the Omega people didn't realize where they got their own energy system!

Then one night I was in the back of a car with some other

people going to an Omega event. And lo and behold I started receiving telepathic communications. At first I thought I was imagining things, but the voices kept talking to me, identifying themselves by different initials that I had never heard of. I wasn't very familiar with the different masters at that point. Then one of them said, "We want to send you this energy." And I said, "What?" And they just repeated themselves. So the first shaktipat with telepathic communication that I ever received from a spiritual master was in the back seat of a car. Later on I ran the energy on other people, and was given directions on how to "lock it in," so I locked it in. The people could feel it, and they were greatly moved by the very profound and beautiful energy. It was actually a precursor to the Drisana energy, starting to build up my subtle body so I could receive more advanced energies.

VE: Let me interrupt a moment and ask you to explain the terms "ran the energy" and "locked it in."

IF: Running energy means being a pipeline for having the energy pass through you and into someone else temporarily. It's not your personal energy, it's divine energy. So when you run energy on someone it comes through you, and it passes through them. It can effect them very profoundly, but it's not there permanently. If you lock energy into someone, that energy remains with them permanently, and they in turn can have the capacity to access that energy at any time that they want to. Then they could run it on someone else. But they could not lock it into someone else unless they were given that ability. So running is temporary and locking-in is permanent.

VE: And to which portion of their beingness does the energy come when you run it, and where is it locked in?

IF: That's a good question. Different energies are locked-in at different levels. There are different levels to the human aura, different levels to our energy fields. Depending on the nature of the energy and what it does, it's locked-in at different energy levels.

VE: There is a multiplicity of levels...

IF: Yes. More than most people realize. I have been given the information that follows by T.K., who is a Tibetan master who is actually in a body. He wasn't born into that body; it is something called a mayavirupa, which is to say the body of manifestation. A master can simply materialize a body. T.K. is the source of many of the energies that we work with in the S.U.N. The information, which I have from him, is that there are 32 levels in the human aura if you count the physical body as one of the levels. Most aura books show only the first few of those 32 because most people aren't clairvoyant enough to perceive that the latter ones exist. Each one exists at a higher vibration level than the one below it. And as you move out, it becomes progressively more difficult to tune in to that subtle body.

VE: So these energy fields extend from the physical body out into what we would call air or space beyond us. How many do you see, and what does that mean to you?

IF: Well, I can sense all 32 of them, but it becomes harder to sense them in great detail past about 17. There are different names for these subtle bodies. The names that I use are, from the inside out, the etheric body, the emotional body, the mental body and the next layer out is what I call the causal body. Most people, including clairvoyants, aren't perceiving beyond the causal body in one lifetime. Many times when people think they are, they are really perceiving different levels or layers *within* the causal body. You see, each subtle body has different frequency subdivisions within it. The causal body is more spiritual than the first three subtle bodies (the etheric, emotional and mental) but less purely spiritual compared to the ones which come after it. The causal body is key because it's a bridge between the lower bodies and the higher bodies that come after it. By "after" I mean that they are further out in space as you move from the physical body outward.

VE: But those layers do interpenetrate one another.

IF: Agreed. All the subtle bodies do finally come down into the physical body. They are not as shown in some aura books or chakra books where they appear as concentric shells or ovals—separate from each other. As you see in **Illustration#1**, they are distinctive but also interpenetrating from the outer to the inner.

Illustration #1 - As we move out from the physical body, the first four subtle bodies are the etheric (which vitalizes the physical), the emotional, the mental, and the causal (which is spiritually oriented). These four subtle bodies interpenetrate each other, as well as the physical body.

It is true that each subtle body is strongest at a particular region in space and if you look at the region where they're strongest, it does look like separated regions. That's why many people don't perceive that each subtle body goes down into the physical body. Your emotional subtle body is not just a shell that is floating out in space separated from you. It comes down into the physical body. How can it be otherwise? We know that when we experience our emotions, we experience the flow of energy down in the physical body. So the emotional body, or what some people call the astral body, penetrates down into the physical.

All of these subtle bodies overlap each other, and are superimposed upon each other, and they exist in the same region in space. However, it is true that as we go from the body outward, each subtle body is strongest in a certain portion in space. This is because the subtle bodies are wave fronts, standing wave fronts. There are a lot of what physicists call "destructive interference" between the subtle bodies. "Destructive" (as used here) doesn't have any negative connotation to it. It simply means that certain frequencies tend to cancel each other out. This is what makes each subtle body strongest in a certain region in space. Yet they all go down into the physical body. That is why energy attunements that go into one of the higher spiritual bodies can affect you physically, emotionally, and mentally, because they come down and interpenetrate the lower bodies, including the dense physical.

VE: People talk about souls or their higher selves—their inner being or the greater part of themselves—as the influence of guidance in their life. Do these exist in the subtle body fields?

IF: The soul definitely manifests through the subtle body fields, but should not be equated with them. The key subtle body for unifying the personality and soul is the causal body. Let me explain this further by talking about some ideas from the Theosophical tradition, which offers teachings about the nature of reality and the nature of our energy fields that come to us from a Spiritual Hierarchy. In the Theosophical view, human beings are really three-part beings. There is what is called a monad, which is the ultimate source of our identity. The ultimate sense of our I AM presence comes from the monad. And then there is the soul, which issues forth from the monad. Finally there is the personality, which issues forth from the soul. D.K. tells us in the Alice Bailey writings that the soul is neither matter nor spirit; the soul is the intermediary between the two. That concept has been stated many times throughout history, from ancient times to modern times. So in terms of the subtle bodies...well, let me step back a minute.

There are two arcs of creation in the universe. There is what is called the involutionary arc and the evolutionary arc. The involutionary arc is the descent of spirit into matter, and it has been called the out-breath of God. The evolutionary arc is the ascent of matter into spirit. It has been called the in-breath of God. The soul is the dynamic principle that allows those arcs to interact, to intersect with each other. The soul is engaged in a process of *descent*. It needs to learn to come down into the lower vehicles (physical, emotional, and mental bodies) and express itself through the lower vehicles. The personality is engaged in a process of *ascent*, of learning to rise in vibrational rate, to rise in consciousness. As I mentioned before, the body that plays the role of a bridge is the causal body. It is more spiritual than the three lower bodies—the etheric, the emotional and the mental—that represent the physical, emotional and mental aspects of a personality. It is less spiritual than the bodies that come after it. So the influence of the soul is particularly important in affecting the causal body. There is always a *lot* of soul energy present in the causal body. Our job as human beings, from an energy perspective, is to learn how to bring down the soul energy, which is always present in the causal body, and integrate that into the physical, emotional, and mental bodies and aspects of personality. This involves releasing a lot of resistance on the physical, emotional and mental levels.

VE: So when you view a human being, being

clairvoyant as you are, what is it that you see that helps you determine or know what kind of an energy flow you should give someone?

IF: Basically, it's contact with my soul. I am what some people call "soul-clairvoyant." There is an important distinction between ordinary clairvoyance, which is the clairvoyance that most people—even most professional clairvoyants—are operating from, and soul-clairvoyance. Ordinary clairvoyance is a power of the personality to see, whereas soul-clairvoyance is being able to see with the eyes of the *soul*. From a practical perspective, ordinary clairvoyance will limit you to certain frequencies of subtle energy.

VE: Because…?

IF: Because the structures of the personality, including our own energy fields, can cause limitations. It is important to realize that spiritual energy, subtle energy in general, just like physical energy, exists at many different frequencies. There is not just one frequency of energy. This makes total sense if you think about it. The frequencies of energy that a human being needs are very different than the frequencies that a plant or an animal needs. So if you talk to different clairvoyants, or look in different books about clairvoyance, you will find that people usually describe different layers of auras having different colors, or two clairvoyants might look at the same person and they will describe different colors in the aura of the same person. That's because they are operating from ordinary clairvoyance. Each one is seeing certain frequencies of subtle energies that are there, but not seeing others. If you have fully developed soul-clairvoyance, then you can see all the frequencies that exist. Basically, you can see what your soul wants you to see. In practice, even human beings who are soul clairvoyant are not fully developed. People need to remember that even soul clairvoyants don't see everything and that they can make mistakes.

We as human beings are superimpositions of many different vibrational levels. For instance, there is the chakra system and the meridian system, and they exist at different vibrational levels. This answers a question which otherwise is quite puzzling. If you look at the Hindu tradition, you find that there is this incredibly detailed knowledge about chakras, even the description of the number of petals on each chakra, to the functioning and the color of each petal. (For a good description of the chakras, please see page 74.) But you find essentially no description of the meridian system or of acupuncture points. How is it possible that some of the wisest men and women, some of the most clairvoyant and insightful men and women who ever lived, missed the meridian system?

On the other hand, if you look at the Taoist tradition, you find the most incredible knowledge about the meridians, lines of energy flow, which are not just straight, but zig-zaggy lines. You couldn't guess in advance what those lines look like. Yet the Taoists described hundreds and hundreds of acupuncture points throughout the body. Even so, Taoism has virtually no description of the chakra system. How is it that some of the wisest and most clear-seeing men and women who have ever lived could see the meridian system yet miss the chakra system? The answer is that *the chakra system and the meridian system exist in different vibrational spaces.*

Let me give an analogy to explain what I mean by a vibrational space. Let's say you are out in the countryside on a beautiful day, and you shut your eyes. You are just aware of sounds. You can hear the birds singing but you don't see anything. You are in a certain vibrational realm that exists only at the level of sound. On the other hand, supposing you then open your eyes and cover up your ears so that you see things but don't hear things. The world seems totally different. You are in the vibrational realm of light, which exists at a different vibrational frequency all together than sound. It is like you are in a whole different space, as we say, a whole different world or realm of being.

And there are still other realms. You see, in modern Western society people who do energy work tend to think primarily in terms of chakras and meridians, but there is more to life than chakras and meridians. If you go to the Middle East, you will find that they work with what are called "lat'if." If you go to Hawaii, you will find that they work with what are called the "ao," which literally means "realm." In Kaballah they work with the "sefirot" or "Tree of Life" centers. Now, I have seen people try to equate the Tree of Life centers with the chakras. That is simply not true. They exist in different vibrational realms. If you're clairvoyant enough you can see that chakras and Tree of Life centers have very different internal structures. Some centers in these different vibrational realms exist in the same geometrical space, but they exist in different vibrational spaces. *It is very important to realize that two centers can occupy the same geometrical space and be in an entirely different vibrational space.*

Everyone's been in a room that has one geometrical space but which contains many different vibrational realms such as the vibrational realm of light, the vibrational realm of sound, and many others that most people are simply not aware of. Similarly, when we go into the spiritual realm, there are innumerable vibrational realms there, more than most people commonly recognize.

VE: So are you saying that most of the really influential spiritual realms are non-sensory to the average person; that we can't identify them and can't realize that they are there?

IF: Definitely! That's why it is possible to be an atheist, as I was for many years, because you can live in this world and be totally immersed in its lower levels, and not be aware that higher spiritual frequencies exist.

VE: So you could be, shall we say, unconscious and unaware?

IF: That's right. And what is equally important to realize is that you can be aware of one vibrational realm within the spiritual world, and be totally unaware of other vibrational realms within the spiritual world, just as some people in the physical world are totally unaware of the spiritual realm altogether.

VE: For instance, someone could be so immersed in

loving Jesus or the Buddha, or in some feminine energy—
Mother Mary, Kwan Yin, etc.—that they would be very
committed to those energies their whole life long. Would that
necessarily be a wise thing?

IF: Well, I wouldn't call it good or bad. I would say that
it is incomplete. I believe it's God's intention that eventually,
over many reincarnations, people will become aware of
multiple spiritual realms.

We are all playing what I call the cosmic forgetting game.
We are all manifestations of God, and when we are born we
lose track of that. One of the important goals of our lives, in
fact, really *the* most important goal in our life, is to become
aware of that broader spectrum of multiple spiritual realms.

What many people don't realize is that this forgetting
game exists not only at an individual level, but also at a
societal level. So Buddhism, for example, just to pick one
tradition at random, has very important truths and insights—
which Hinduism doesn't have. But the converse is equally true.
Hinduism has very important insights and truths, which Buddhism doesn't have. And we could go on and on. The Navajo
and Hopi traditions have insights which neither Hinduism
nor Buddhism have. Each of us has a piece of the puzzle.

The analogy that I like to use is that Source (which I would
call God) resembles a very beautiful infinitely-faceted jewel.
And each tradition is looking at just one facet of that jewel.
The problem comes when you start thinking that the facet you
are looking at is the only one.

VE: Yes, violent wars are fought over these issues, aren't
they?

IF: Very sadly so. Now from an energetic perspective
what happens is that *when you have certain key categories of energies in your body from different traditions, different shaktis, these
energies mix and certain elixirs start to manifest*, which propel
your spiritual evolution in an extraordinary way. So it is not
just a philosophical point that different traditions have different parts of the puzzle, different parts of this jewel. It is also
very important from a very practical viewpoint that we

experience key energies from different traditions in our physical, emotional, mental, causal and other bodies. We are all part of an evolutionary process that is incomplete. We now know from brain wave studies that the advanced states of consciousness accessed by different spiritual traditions, though similar, also have important differences. There is a step that goes beyond people coming to enlightenment within different traditions, within Christianity, within Buddhism, within Taoism, within Hinduism, within Huna, etc. There is a step beyond each where we integrate the knowledge, the consciousness, and the energies of these different traditions. This process of integration is one of the important long-range goals of the S.U.N.

VE: When did you move from your personal experience of the energies to the realization that you needed to do some kind of organizational dispensation for humanity or groups of people?

IF: It was definitely an evolutionary process. I started out approaching this just because of my own personal health needs. And then I began meeting in groups with other people to share the energy work.

As a result of seeing the profound effect that these energies had, not just on myself but also on other people, I became really convinced that it was important that these initiations be made generally available to the public.

Then, as I was walking along one day, T.K. said, "That is not just an idle thought. Your soul-purpose is to found an organization that will make these different initiations available to the public—not just the initiations from one tradition, but the initiations from multiple traditions. And then to go a step beyond that, to integrate the work of the different traditions into a more coherent whole."

VE: That must have been an exciting moment in your life.

IF: It was! It was very exciting, but at first I also had a great deal of personality resistance to this because it's a lot of work. And to be honest, I didn't want to do it. I simply didn't want to get involved. I could see the great difficulty of starting an organization that would deal with people's resistance to realizing how many different wonderful energies there are and to show them there is an interrelationship between these energies. At first I tried getting teachers from other organizations involved so I wouldn't have to be the primary person. I wanted to pass along the information that I was receiving and get someone else to take it from there. When that didn't work I had to become a willing participant and move ahead myself.

VE: How long has the S.U.N. organization been going now?

IF: It's been in existence since 1992, so the Spiritual Unfoldment Network is a fairly young organization.

VE: Like most of us, you had to begin the process of willingness and then let that flow into the world, organize it, and have the right people come forth to be with you…right?

IF: Yes. Once I began doing this, I found that it developed an extraordinary momentum of its own. First it started with just me being the only S.U.N. teacher putting this information out there, and it was very hard work. I would give about three lectures a week, typically in my living room at night. Very often at the start no one would come. Then there would just be a couple of people. Then more people started coming and the organization began to develop momentum. I found that once it became known that I was engaged in that type of enterprise, there was something about the material which captured people's imagination. The work become much easier. The hard part is getting started. You know the saying that when the student is ready the teacher will appear. Well, the flip side of it is that when you are teaching something that is truly of the light, then the students will appear. I would encourage anyone who is reading these words, who is doing such work and is having slow going at first, to stick with it. Eventually you will find that people will be there because we humans are far more energy-oriented than we presently realize.

VE: I want to acknowledge that I really experienced

something special when I met you for the first time at the Whole Life Exposition in San Francisco. You did a talk on "Esoteric Energy Work from Around the World." What was the energy you sent to all of us that day?

IF: Well at different times I do different energies. It might have been an energy called Heart Light.

VE: Whatever it was, I had a personal experience in my heart of a spark of light as real as if somebody had just sat there and touched me directly. So even though you were sitting quietly up in the front of the room, not saying a word, just sending, I experienced the energy. I have been close to people where they have to touch you on the forehead in order to send that physical expression of shakti. But I never had it zipped across a big room with several hundred people in it. So I knew that you were in control of something extraordinary. From that very personal experience I felt guided to contact you, and we have since come to know each other. So how are you able to transmit energy so strongly?

IF: The key is I really open up to my soul and my Solar Angel. I talked a little bit about the soul previously. The Solar Angel is what some people refer to as the guardian angel. I prefer the term "Solar Angel" for various reasons. The main reason is that the function of the guardian angel is not really to guard you, although it does do that. But some of the things that the personality most wants to guard against are things that your Solar Angel most wants you to experience. The primary purpose of the Solar Angel is to oversee your personal and spiritual evolution. *The existence of the Solar Angel is one of the single most important things a person can realize.* Working with the Solar Angel is one of the most important and beautiful things that anyone can do. The existence of the Solar Angel is what theosophist Helena Blavatsky called the "Secret of the Ages." It is at the core of many of the ancient mystery school teachings. So the soul and the Solar Angel together constitute what people call the Higher Self.

Many people work with the Higher Self without realizing this. You don't have to realize it in order to work with the

Higher Self, but once you understand this, there are many other steps that you can take. The Higher Self really consists of our soul, which is a part of ourselves, and our Solar Angel, which is a separate being. Then it's really through surrender to the Higher Self, through the soul and the Solar Angel working together in intimate union, that the most advanced forms of energy work are possible. People who want to learn more about the extraordinarily close relationship between the soul and the Solar Angel can read the teachings of D.K. in the Alice Bailey books.

People often ask me, "Well, how can you do all these things? I've never seen anyone else do things like this." The answer is that "I" am not doing it, if by "I" one means the personality. Basically, I am surrendering to the Higher Self, which ultimately means surrendering to God, and letting the vision and the energies of the Higher Self come through the personality.

If you are dependent on the vision of the personality, you will see certain frequencies and not others. If you can see with the eyes of the Higher Self, then you can see whatever the Higher Self wants you to see, and you can see it instantly. I have had sessions with people who have had incarnations in a culture with which I was totally unfamiliar. Though unfamiliar, I was able to work with energy centers that were new to me. I've often talked about how there is much more than chakras and meridians—how there are many different energy centers. To give a more concrete example, somebody might be sitting in front of me, and I might be clairvoyantly seeing the standard things, such as the layers of the aura, the chakras, and the meridians. Then my Higher Self might say to me, "This person had an incarnation in such-and-such obscure culture," perhaps one that I never even heard of before. "They worked with certain energy centers that you're not familiar with, and here's what they look like." And then, bang! Instantly I will see the entire set of centers, the entire set of channels in that person, but you can't do this if you see only with the vision of the personality.

VE: Tell me more about what you actually experience and see.

IF: When I look at someone I see the different layers of the aura, I see the chakras, I see the meridians. I see the Tree of Life centers, and I see the "ao," which incidentally are very much related to the Tree of Life centers. These are all things that I have worked with and that I am familiar with. It's not that my personality disappears, it's still there. Yet while I see the things that my personality is used to seeing I rely on my Higher Self for all the additional information, implications, and anything beyond what my personality sees. What is taking place is integration between the personality and the Higher Self. Perhaps I should use the word "soul" in this context. A lot of spiritual evolution is involved with what in the Western mystery school tradition is called "personality-soul fusion." The personality and the soul need to become integrated. The soul doesn't come in and replace the personality, or banish the personality. When many people talk about spiritual evolution they talk as though some higher principle were to come in and transcend or replace the personality. The soul needs the personality as much as the personality needs the soul.

VE: So you are now able to utilize your earthly personality and your expanded personality-soul fusion to be of service?

IF: Yes. Certainly my abilities are also related to my particular talents. A person may be very evolved spiritually, but that doesn't necessarily mean that they are automatically able to play the violin. My own personality has a talent for working with energy. That's certainly a part of it, but I emphasize the role of the Higher Self because that is really the key to doing advanced energy work. I have seen many cases of people who were operating at a fraction of their potential because they were coming from the personality, primarily, rather than surrendering to the Higher Self. The truth is that you could spend your entire life studying the subtle bodies, and only understand a fraction of what there is to know. The complexity of energy anatomy far transcends what most people realize. It certainly far transcends the capacity of the human intellect to understand it all. If you look at the average book about auras and chakras and so forth, the amount of information that is present is a fraction of the amount of information that you see in a standard first year medical book about human physical anatomy. Now the truth is that subtle anatomy is far more complicated than physical anatomy, so this gives you an idea of how much material is missing.

VE: Well, hopefully, those who are healers, or who are interested in energy work of some kind (either at a spiritual, mental, emotional, or physical level) will be open to receiving and understanding more about energy through willingness and commitment.

IF: I certainly hope so! Let me make it clear, I am not talking about throwing away our intellect. I am not talking about throwing out personal intuition. Those things have a place, an important place, but to make an analogy with a symphony orchestra, they shouldn't be the conductors. The Higher Self should be the conductor. All of these other things should play in the orchestra, under the direction of the Higher Self. When we realize just how complex things are, and then surrender to the Higher Self, we can really accomplish the most in our everyday lives. Today you can walk into a room and flip on a light switch, and it's quite miraculous. The average person today has access to more energy than the greatest kings and queens of ancient times. But how many people can understand the wiring? If you were to take it apart, pull off the light switch cover, how many people would understand the wiring that's behind there?

VE: But if you are an electrician, it's essential to know.

IF: If you're an electrician, it's helpful. But we don't need to understand it. Similarly, we don't need to know everything about energy anatomy to do really effective energy work. For most people it takes many, many years to develop the kind of union with the Higher Self I've been talking about, but anyone can receive an initiation to use shakti. Shakti is the gift of divine grace from God, and through working with shakti, you can do deeper and more powerful work on your chakras, for example, than you can by spending your entire lifetime understanding the chakras. So it's just like on the daily life level, we can accomplish much more when we realize that we are part of an interconnected network, that we are not alone. When I flip on the light switch, I am relying on the knowledge of electricians and all the information they have developed over time. Well, why not rely on the knowledge of God?

VE: Now this brings up the motives of why people would want to learn about energy. We understand that this is an integrity issue, a moral issue for humanity, since there's been misuse of the energies. What would you say about your position as one who is able to utilize these energies, without the structure of a specific religion? When you help someone with energy, where does the responsibility lie if they decide to go off and use that in a negative way? How do you view your relationship with the general public in these moral and ethical matters?

IF: Well, part of my work is not just to give people energies, but to educate them about surrender to the Higher Self, which is ultimately surrender to God. The problems that we have with the abuse of energy come from the personality level, of course, not from the soul level. One of the things that I require of all of the S.U.N. teachers, is that they actually sign a written contract in which they agree to surrender to their Higher Self. Actually in the contract it specifies that the guardian angel, or what I call the Solar Angel, has permission to prevent inappropriate uses of energy, including stopping energy transmissions.

VE: So in other words, in a simple and straightforward clarity, you are advising people that it is possible to avoid misuse of energy through the protection of their own Higher Self?

IF: It is, yes. However, this is only a partial solution to this problem because the primary directive of the spiritualrealm, including the angelic kingdom, is that they must respect human free will. The contract gives the Higher Self permission to intervene, but it doesn't automatically guarantee that it will intervene because sometimes we must have our freedom to make certain mistakes. So this is only a partial solution, but it really is the best solution that I have been able to come up with. I have seen the effects of this agreement and I believe it actually works. But there can't really be a complete solution to this problem because as human beings we have free will. Looking at it from another perspective, even though we might regret abuses of energy that we've seen, it's a good thing that there isn't a solution to this problem. If there were it would imply that we didn't have free will. This is the most precious gift that God has given all sentient beings.

VE: So it's important, then, for each individual, before they would come to you for courses or for other assistance, to simply know that you and the S.U.N. organization have this point of view.

IF: Yes, and in certain particular courses, which develop supernormal abilities that can be abused, I require this contract. This contract is not one I require of students in general, but it is what I require of the S.U.N. teachers, and it is one which I have signed myself...as have you.

VE: Is there anything else about your organization or yourself that you want to share in this particular interview?

IF: What I want to say about the role of the Spiritual Unfoldment Network is that our purpose is to make certain energy work tools available, which can dramatically accelerate people's personal and spiritual evolution. When I say "dramatically" I mean that quite literally. Most people are familiar with the energies that are most commonly available, not with the energies that are the most powerful. However, we do this in a way that respects people's free will. We're not here to tell people how they have to lead their lives or what they must believe. When someone takes our courses, there is support that is available afterwards. We have meetings to which people can come and share energy work, and can ask questions of the teacher who taught their course. People are always free to call up their teacher, so support is there. However, if someone wants to come to one of our classes and receive the initiations and go home and use the energy afterwards for themselves or for their friends, and never talk to us again, that's fine. Our primary purpose is to educate people about shakti.

VE: Because, you said, that T.K. had some very clear motives for asking you to assist in that process...

IF: There are really two general categories as to why we are doing what we are doing. One is to make the energy work available because of the profound effect it can have for accelerating personal and spiritual evolution. The other reason has a more planetary aspect to it—to prepare for the coming of the World Teacher. What T.K. has told me many times in these exact words is, "Initiate as many people as quickly as possible." The idea is to raise the consciousness and shift the energy field of as many people as possible, so that when the World Teacher next appears, the world will be more ready to receive him or her. Now when I say World Teacher, it's what some people in the West refer to as the "Christ." Other people use different terms. In Buddhism they talk about Maitreya Buddha. In Islam, they talk about the Imam Mahdi. You see, everyone's waiting for someone. Different people have different names for this person, but the truth is that it is the same great spiritual guide.

The World Teacher is not going to appear just for Christians or just for Buddhists, or any one group. The World Teacher is coming for everyone.

Chapter 3

ENERGY

Conversation between Virginia and Irving

VE: Many of the topics we discuss in this book relate, directly or indirectly, to subtle energy. This is a difficult concept for many people because it is usually defined as being "non-physical" and they either don't understand what this means or they don't see how something which is itself non-physical can have tangible effects. Will you comment on this?

IF: First let me define what I mean when I use the term "subtle energy." When we use the word "subtle" in ordinary language, it can refer to something which is difficult to detect. Similarly, I would define a subtle energy as one which cannot currently be detected by mainstream scientific instruments. The situation we're in with subtle energy is analogous to the early days of research into electricity. At that time experimenters observed that frog legs hanging from a rack would jump when the rack was hit with lightning; however, they had no understanding of electricity and no way of measuring it. We can observe effects of subtle energy, but we don't yet have standard scientific instruments for measuring and quantifying it. One day we will have such instruments and then subtle energy will be considered just as real as any other form of energy.

It appears that subtle energies, or at least many of them, don't have any mass. This makes it difficult for some people to understand how such energies can have tangible effects. However, I would like to point out that a photon (a particle of light) also has no mass. Yet bombardment by a stream of photons can produce very real effects. Many readers may have seen solar-powered discs, glass globes with parts which rotate when they are exposed to sunlight, or entry ways utilizing photoelectric beams. Even though photons have no mass they can cause matter to move over a distance or to do "work." In a similar way, even if subtle energy has no mass, it can still do work.

VE: Your use of the word "work" reminds me of the standard scientific definition of energy, namely "the capacity to do work." Do you believe that this definition also implies to subtle energy?

IF: Definitely! Although the definition you quote is commonplace today, its development was a conceptual breakthrough because it unifies many apparently different phenomenon: heat, light, electricity, gravity, etc. Similarly, this definition unifies both the concepts of physical energy and subtle energy. There is a unity to the universe; physical energy and subtle energy obey similar principles. For example, both physical energies and subtle energies have frequencies and amplitudes.

The most important work that subtle energy can do is to produce changes in ourselves. For example the initiations given in this book can lead to changes. To put things in more spiritual terms we could say that energy is the capacity to produce change or transformation.

VE: Now that we've mentioned the similarities between physical energy and subtle energy, what are some of the differences?

IF: Well, one example which illustrates both similarities and differences between physical and subtle energies is that of distant transmission. Like physical energies, subtle energies can be transmitted over large distances. Some readers may be familiar with studies on the distant healing effects of prayer; these have been described in books by Larry Dossey and many others. Also, there are spiritual teachers, both Eastern and Western, who allow some of their energy initiations to be done at a distance.

However, subtle energies appear to travel at speeds which can not be matched by physical energies. It is commonly thought that subtle energies can travel faster than light, which may seem strange to some readers. Nonetheless, a variety of explanations have been proposed by reputable scientists as to how this could happen. One of the most commonly discussed models has been proposed by William Tiller, a Professor Emeritus and former head of the department of Material Sciences and Engineering at Stanford University. I'm not a physicist, but as I understand it, Tiller's model describes electromagnetic waves as transverse waves and subtle energy waves as longitudinal waves. These subtle energy waves have been compared to pressure waves running longitudinally under the ocean. The velocities of these pressure waves are not limited by the transverse velocities of the surface waves. Readers who are interested in finding out more about Tiller's model can read his book <u>Science and Human Transformation: Subtle Energies, Intentionality, and Consciousness</u>. What is intriguing about Tiller's model is that it can be interpreted to mean that the longitudinal subtle energy waves actually create the conventional transverse electromagnetic waves. This is in accord with the ancient spiritual wisdom that the lower vibrational planes of reality are manifested from the higher vibrational planes of reality.

VE: The fact that there are models which explain how subtle energies could travel faster than light might help some readers to understand how an energy initiation could be sent from a being in another star system to the Earth so quickly.

IF: Yes. What I want to emphasize is that regardless of which proposed model of subtle energy turns out to be correct, we are talking about something for which we will ultimately find a scientific explanation. We routinely use modes of communication which would have seemed like magic to our distant ancestors: radio, satellite transmissions, etc. Arthur C. Clarke said that any sufficiently advanced technology looks like magic. The technology behind the subtle energy initiations in this book is very advanced indeed. It may look like magic, but like all subtle energy phenomenon it obeys rational principles.

VE: What are some other differences between physical energy and subtle energy?

IF: There are two other interrelated differences which I would like to mention. The first is that subtle energy responds much more readily to human consciousness than physical energy. An everyday example is how a thought can be transformed into bodily motion, such as moving a finger. In Taoism they would say thought moves the chi and the chi moves the body.

A related concept is that subtle energy can be "programmed." Readers may be familiar with programming a quartz crystal, for example. Of course, what is really being programmed is the subtle energy field associated with the crystal.

The fact that subtle energy can be programmed leads us to the concept of "shakti." A shakti is a subtle energy which has been programmed to behave intelligently, either directly by God (some people may prefer to use another word, such as Source) or indirectly by an intermediary (such as an Ascended Master or angel) who is so spiritually evolved that they can act as a pure pipeline for the divine mind. The word shakti expresses the concept that energy is God in action. Unfortunately, there isn't even an English word to describe this concept; that is why we use the term shakti, which is a Hindu word. Some people in Western culture use the word shakti simply as a synonym for "energy"; however, I always use it to refer to "a subtle energy that behaves intelligently."

VE: So you're distinguishing between the concept of subtle energy and the concept of a shakti?

IF: Yes, a shakti is a specialized form of subtle energy. All shaktis are subtle energies, but not all subtle energies are shaktis. It is common for shakti and ordinary subtle energy to be found mixed together for they frequently act in concert to support our evolution in ways that we can't sort out. I use the phrase "subtle energy" to include the possibility that we are talking about shakti as well as ordinary subtle energy.

We can receive the benefits of a mix of shakti and ordinary subtle energy without having to know which is which. What is important is that we know when we are receiving a shakti. All of the initiations in this book work because they employ shakti.

VE: The subject of shakti is clearly one of great importance. I am sure that many readers will be surprised they haven't heard more about this subject previously.

IF: In our culture we commonly think of energy only in a very physical way. Spiritual understandings about energy have been present in many other cultures (particularly Eastern cultures) for thousands of years. However, they are still in the process of becoming more widely known in our own culture. These spiritual concepts lie behind all of the initiations in this book. They also have much broader applicability to more than just the initiations in this book.

Western culture is still in its infancy in learning about subtle energy and about the energy centers already known in other cultures. For historical reasons the West learned about chakras and meridians first, and as a result, many people have assumed that this is all that there is to know, or all that is important.

We still have much to learn from these cultures with which we already have the most familiarity. For example, in Hinduism there is a vast knowledge not only of the chakras but also of the energy centers known as marmas. These are located in regions where bones, joints, muscles, ligaments, blood vessels, or nerves meet. These centers are important concentrations of life energy. As mentioned, we also have much to learn from traditions that are not as familiar to us. Sufism has knowledge about the energy centers known as lat'if, the Jewish tradition of Kabbalah has knowledge about the energy centers known as sefirot (or the Tree of Life centers), and the Hawaiian tradition of Huna knows about centers called ao. Experience has shown that combining knowledge of the chakras and meridians with work on any of these other energy centers, produces results that far exceed what can be done by working with just the chakras and meridians alone. To master knowledge of all these different centers is beyond the capacity of any human intelligence; however, through the medium of shakti it becomes possible to work with these less known centers in a very profound way.

It is important to understand, as stated previously, that a shakti is a subtle energy, not a physical energy. It is also important to understand that it is not anyone's personal energy (for example, the shaktis associated with the initiations in this book are not the personal energies of the authors nor are they the personal energies of the masters from whom you can receive these initiations.)

Although the concept of a shakti may be new to many people, each of us experiences these energies on a daily basis. They fill the entire universe. Indeed, it is the presence of these energies which is the immediate cause of the magnificent design and order which we see throughout life. Shakti acts at all levels of reality. It gives a direction to the physical evolution of the universe, to biological evolution, and to our own personal and spiritual evolution. And shakti is the everyday work tool of spirit.

VE: Can you give us an example of what you mean by "the everyday work tool of spirit?"

IF: One example is that many prayers are answered on God's behalf by spiritual beings (such as angels) using shakti. Before I elaborate on that statement, I need to explain two general principles. First: Although the spiritual realm has the power to answer our prayers by changing our external circumstances, it would prefer to facilitate our inner growth and empower us to change those circumstances ourselves. Second: Every state of consciousness is associated with a corresponding state in our subtle bodies. If we first bring about the corresponding state in our subtle bodies, we can encourage but not compel that state of consciousness.

Now that I've explained those two points, let's consider

the example of someone who prays for inner strength to meet a life challenge. One way that prayer could be answered is for a spiritual being to use a shakti that helps the person's subtle body energy fields become more like those of a person experiencing inner strength. Using such a shakti respects the person's free will; it encourages change but doesn't force them to change. The person must still do their share of the work; to the extent that they shift their consciousness there is a corresponding resonance in the shakti, and it can facilitate even deeper change. Because shakti behaves intelligently it can personalize what it does to that particular person.

This example also illustrates the fact that when spiritual beings cause change they don't just wave a magic wand and cause things to happen without any intermediary mechanism. Change in the physical world happens through energy exchanges; change in the subtle realm (i.e. the planes of reality above the physical plane) also happens through energy exchanges.

VE: Understood, but that raises another question. If a person can receive benefits from shakti by a direct appeal to God or to the spiritual realm in general, why would it be necessary to receive certain energies from specific intermediaries, such as the non-terrestrial masters who give the initiations discussed in this book?

IF: It is indeed true that certain shaktis must be received through intermediaries. Depending on the frequencies used in the shakti, that intermediary might have to be a physical person such as a guru, might have to be a non-physical spiritual being, or in some cases could be either. There are three general reasons why intermediaries are necessary at all. First, many energies require accompanying detailed information about their significance, how to use them, or important safety precautions. Most people don't have their telepathic abilities developed enough to receive this information. Second, many energies are too powerful to be safely sent directly into the energy field of the recipient. They must be passed to the recipient through the energy fields of an intermediary who has very developed subtle bodies and who acts as a transformer, stepping down the power of the energy and passing it on to the recipient. Third, when we come in contact with an intermediary we can also come in contact with other people and/ or with the wisdom of the spiritual tradition(s) that the intermediary represents. This wisdom is a gift of knowledge from the many generations of people who preceded and gave rise to the intermediary. God's wish for us is that we co-evolve with our loving brothers and sisters, not in isolation.

VE: That brings us to a question about God. When I think of God, I think of a dynamic life-giving spirit—the creative energy behind all being. How does this fit with our present scientific worldview?

IF: Understanding the role of shakti enables us to bridge the gap between the scientific worldview and the spiritual worldview. We know from the second law of thermodynamics in physics that by itself matter moves in a direction of increasing entropy, or increasing disorder. For example, if you don't put effort into straightening up a room it tends to become more disorganized, not neater; a building left unattended will eventually fall into disrepair and crumble, etc. Yet in living things, everywhere we look we see order, growth, and evolution. A human being grows from a few cells to eventually contain millions of cells of many different kinds. How does this happen? How do some cells "know" to become skin cells, other cells "know" to become kidney cells...and on and on. The purely scientific answer is to ascribe this to DNA. But DNA is just a blueprint and cannot by itself build a body any more than the blueprint of a house can build a house. What is the guiding force behind the blueprint of DNA? The answer lies in the concept of shakti.

VE: Are you saying that God and shakti are the same?

IF: No, I am not. Shakti ultimately comes from "Source." By Source we refer to that which is the origin and sustaining power of the universe. Different people have different names for this: "God," "Cosmic Mind," "Tao," etc. Even though a shakti has its ultimate origin in Source and even though it behaves intelligently, it should not be equated with Source. Rather it is a tool which Source allows some to pass on to others; it is a nonphysical tool, but a tool nonetheless. Nor should a shakti be considered a living being, even though its intelligent behavior may at times leave one with that impression. Some people have compared a shakti to a nonphysical computer.

Although a shakti may be passed on to you by a physical teacher or by various non-terrestrial masters, remember that it ultimately comes from Source. It does not ultimately originate with that being, nor is it that being's personal energy. Just as Source has provided the universe with all the necessities to sustain physical growth, so has Source provided us with the gift of these shaktis for our personal and spiritual growth. Our part is to be open to an initiation, receiving the grace of shakti, and having done so, to be active co-participants with the shakti in our personal and spiritual transformation.

When a person receives an initiation, those who are clairvoyant might see a shakti as a stream of energy flowing into their aura or their physical body. Others might experience such a shakti through warmth, tingling, or a sense of activity in their chakras. (See page 74 for a good description on the chakras.) Some people might hear subtle sound, or what some call "divine sound." All shakti contains both divine light and divine sound, though the proportion of each can vary greatly from one shakti to another. The spiritual planes are more unified than the physical and there is not the kind of separation between divine light and divine sound that we see between physical light and physical sound. Still others might experience the shakti only through its effects, such as the clearing (removal in whole or in part) of negative thoughts or feelings, or the presence of positive thoughts and feelings (love, compassion, joy.) It is useful for anyone doing the initiations in this book, but particularly for those who do not see or feel subtle energy, to keep a log of their experiences in order to appreciate fully the reality and extent of the transformations they will be having.

There are three concepts that are the most fundamental to an understanding of shakti:
1. Shakti behaves intelligently.
2. There are many shaktis.
3. Shaktis can be permanently imbued into one's energy field.

SHAKTI BEHAVES INTELLIGENTLY

An example of shakti behaving intelligently would be when a shakti that clears negative emotions will head directly for the particular chakras where those emotions are most stored. The fact that shakti behaves intelligently has many important implications not all of which are obvious. By utilizing shakti we can accomplish far more than we can if we only make use of our individual intelligence. Consider a shakti that works with clearing the chakras. (As we will see later, different shaktis work with different energy centers and accomplish different objectives.) A shakti can act more quickly and can access more information about the structure of the chakras than can any individual working alone. In fact, aura photographs of people who have experienced even 15 or 20 minutes of the more powerful shaktis show chakra changes which surprise even many professional energy workers. In addition to having the power to access vast amounts of detail about the more commonly known energy centers, such as the chakras, shaktis are also able to access information about important but less known centers such as the ao, marmas, lat'if and sefirot.

Even though you can read countless books on chakras, our information in the West is only a fraction of what there is to know. But shakti is intelligent and knows far more than any human being can.

VE: So a shakti knows what an individual needs even when we don't know ourselves.

IF: Yes. Another advantage which the intelligent behavior of shakti gives us is a way to work with our blind spots. All of us, no matter how far along the path we may be, are not seeing important truths about ourselves. If this weren't true, we would be further along than we are! These blind spots are self-perpetuating. For example, consider a person who is afraid of feelings. In doing chakra opening exercises, he or she will probably focus less on those chakras whose opening will evoke more feeling, thus perpetuating their imbalance. However, a shakti is more intelligent than our fears. It facilitates the opening of the chakras and will not succumb to this bias. To give another example, all of us have negative beliefs, which we don't even recognize as such; they are so entrenched that we mistake them for reality itself, rather than a negative perception of reality. However a shakti is more intelligent than our habits. It clears negative thought forms and does not buy into such beliefs. To a shakti, a negative thought form has a low vibrational rate regardless of its particular content.

Because shakti behaves intelligently it has the important ability to customize what it does for each person. For instance, a shakti that has the specific purpose of balancing a person's left-right energy may increase the amount of charge on the left side of one person's body and decrease the charge on the left side of another person's body, depending on the individual's unique pattern of imbalance. The degree of customization can be surprisingly great. Some shaktis that specialize in working on the crown chakra can work individually on each one of the thousand-plus petals of that chakra.

THERE ARE MANY SHAKTIS

The second of the three concepts most fundamental to the understanding of shakti is that there is not just one kind of shakti in the universe; there are many, many different shaktis. Shaktis can be quite different from one another. Those who are clairvoyant enough can see that they have different colors. Those who are very sensitive to the feel of energy recognize different textures such as smoothness or graininess. Another difference is that energies can feel hot or cold, even like electricity. They also move in different geometric configurations: some move in straight lines, some move in circles, some move in spirals, etc.

The reason that these distinctions between energies are of practical importance is that different shaktis do very different things. They work on different centers or channels of the body. To try to do everything with one shakti is like trying to construct a building with only one tool. For example, a shakti could work on just the chakra system, just the meridians, both the chakras and the meridians, or neither the chakras nor the meridians. A shakti might work on only one chakra, such as the brow chakra. Even shaktis that work only on the brow chakra can have different functions. One might help with dream interpretation and another might improve a person's memory. A shakti that works in a general way will do more for you overall, but will typically not do as much on a particular energy center as a shakti which works only on that center.

VE: Since different spiritual traditions focus on different parts of our energy anatomy (e.g. chakras or meridians) I would assume different traditions use different shaktis? Within the same tradition is there usually some kind of overall similarity to the energies of that tradition?

IF: Different spiritual traditions do indeed use different shaktis. Within the same spiritual tradition shaktis do tend to have a certain overall similarity which distinguishes them from the energies of other traditions. In saying this we must recognize the limitation of generalizations and the fact that even energies within the same tradition do show variability.

A person who is sensitive to energy and is familiar with shaktis of different traditions can often recognize, without being told, what tradition a particular energy is associated with. For example, certain Buddhist meditation energies can be recognized by the way in which they help us realize that Cosmic Mind has an infinite, sky-like quality to it. On the other hand, certain energies from the Huna tradition in Hawaii can be recognized by the distinctive way in which they help us realize the oceanic qualities of Cosmic Mind.

Often people find that they have specific patterns in their responses to the energies of different traditions. One person might find that they tend to respond strongly to Buddhist energies but not that much to Hindu energies. Another person might be just the opposite and find that they respond strongly to Hindu energies, but not that much to Buddhist energies. Just as people respond individually to different physical energies such as those in music or food, they respond individually to the energies of different traditions, as well. This is why it is useful for someone interested in exploring the world of energies to investigate energies from different spiritual traditions. The spiritual traditions which one practiced in previous incarnations is one important factor in determining how one will respond to the energies of different traditions in this lifetime.

One of the many wonderful properties of the star initiations in this book is that they work with energy frequencies that are part of *the universal heritage of humanity*. Everyone can benefit from these initiations, regardless of who they are in this lifetime or who they have been in previous lifetimes!

VE: Knowing that there are so many different subtle energies, how can we keep them all straight? Can we group them into categories of some sort?

IF: All the ancient traditions from which Western culture has learned about energy have ways of creating categories for different kinds of energy. To give an example, let's consider some of the distinctions that are made in the Hindu tradition. In Hinduism different human *faculties* are associated with different energies. Intention or will is associated with iccha shakti, action with kriya shakti and knowledge with jnana shakti.

Within the body, different *processes* are associated with different energies. Breathing is governed by the energy called prana, circulation is governed by the energy called vyana, digestion by samana, elimination of wastes by apana, the link between the physical and the spiritual is governed by the energy called udana.

Regarding the *locations* within a physical body, each chakra is governed by a different shakti. The names given to these can vary, but one common set is as follows. The base chakra is governed by Dakini, the sacral chakra by Rakini, the solar plexus chakra by Lakini, the heart chakra by Kakini, the throat chakra by Shakini, the brow chakra by Hakimi, and the crown chakra by Chaitanya. Many other illustrations of distinctions in Hinduism could be given but those related above illustrate the point.

We could also mention distinctions made in other cultures, such as in the Hawaiian tradition of Huna, where different qualities of physical light in nature are associated with various kinds of subtle/spiritual energy. The distinctions between different kinds of energies are not idle ones. It is not possible to have a truly comprehensive science of subtle energy if all energies are considered the same, anymore than it is possible to have a science of chemistry if all the elements are considered to be the same.

VE: How is it that the knowledge of these distinctions has been lost in modern America and elsewhere?

IF: One answer has to do with some characteristics of modern Western culture, particularly recent American culture. Too often we are looking for the easy answer, the quick fix. In New Age culture many students flit from one course to another superficially, without ever applying the knowledge or ever stopping to really study the ancient wisdom from which the knowledge of the energies is derived. Although the study of this ancient wisdom is a process that may take many years, the rewards are well worth it!

Perhaps another answer has to do with the fact that the English language lacks a vocabulary for describing different kinds of energy. As a result people have often relied on the use of the phrase "universal life energy." This phrase contains within it the seed for a serious misunderstanding. If you look up the word "universal" you will find that it means "present everywhere." It does not mean "unique." Thus, in the physical realm, we could say that heat is "universal physical energy" since it is present throughout the universe. However, it would be equally correct to say that gravitational energy is "universal physical energy." But they are not the same. Just as there are many different physical energies, there are many different subtle energies. One way to see this is from the fact that different minerals have unique metaphysical energies. The properties of amethyst are by no means the same as those of rose quartz. If there were only one kind of subtle energy in the universe, then all minerals would be putting out just that one energy and all minerals would have the same metaphysical properties. Similarly, different flower essences have different metaphysical properties, whereas if there were only one subtle energy in the universe all flowers would have the same metaphysical properties.

VE: But all these different subtle energies still come from the same Source, don't they?

IF: Of course. I have emphasized the diversity of subtle energy to help balance out a tendency in the New Age movement to greatly oversimplify reality and talk only about "universal life energy." However, because I have emphasized this diversity, I want to affirm that *ultimately* there is an underlying unity to all energies, both physical and subtle, for all energies ultimately come from the one Source which creates and sustains the universe. Nonetheless, it is a mistake to assume that this ultimate unity means that all subtle energies are identical.

To realize the ultimate oneness of the universe is a beautiful and profoundly uplifting experience. We can maintain our belief in that oneness without having to assume all energies are identical, just as we don't assume all people are identical, even though we all ultimately originate from Source. Indeed, the fact that the "One" manifests as the "many" is itself a source of great beauty. Accepting the fact that there are so many different kinds of energy can be difficult if you have not encountered this teaching previously. However, understanding this diversity is both enriching and empowering. Just as our lives are both enriched and empowered by the many manifestations of physical light such as red, orange, and yellow, etc., so our lives are both enriched and empowered by the many manifestations of spiritual light.

VE: So, knowing that shakti is intelligent and that there are many different shaktis—more than we can count—what is that third important concept about shakti?

SHAKTIS CAN BE PERMANENTLY INSTALLED INTO YOUR ENERGY FIELD

IF: Our third concept about shakti is that it is possible to have your subtle energy fields imbued with a permanent shakti initiation from another being—sometimes an embodied being and sometimes a non-physical spiritual being. However, receiving a personal shakti initiation does *not* empower you to initiate someone else or to pass that shakti to others, for this is an entirely different matter. Also, each initiation uses only one particular shakti. In some traditions there are rituals or practices which you must do after receiving the initiation in order to receive the benefits of the shakti, such as mantras or visualization. In other cases, such as the initiations in this book, there is no specific ritual or ongoing practice that you need to do in order to experience the benefit of the shakti. Still, in all cases, it is most helpful for us to be open to change and to be active co-participants with the shakti in our personal and spiritual growth.

Remember that whenever you receive an initiation you do so, not in isolation, but as an individual living on a planet. Every human being is intimately connected to Mother Earth. Indeed, the evolution of humanity as a whole and the evolution of planet Earth are inextricably intertwined. Acceleration in either evolutionary process must eventually result in an acceleration of the other; a block in either evolutionary process must eventually result in a block in the other. We can better comprehend why this is so by understanding the structure and functioning of the Earth's gridwork system.

First, let me clarify what I mean by the term "Earth's gridwork." Some people have used this term in discussing physical, electromagnetic energy. The term "Earth's gridwork" has also been used—as we use it in this book—to refer to a system of *channels* which are made up of subtle (not physical) matter and which conduct the flow of subtle (not physical) energy. A good way to understand the Earth is by analogy with a human being. A human being has a physical body and also has a nested sequence of subtle bodies, which interpenetrate and surround the physical body. Similarly, the Earth has a physical body and also has a nested sequence of subtle bodies, which interpenetrate and surround that physical Earth. The Earth's gridwork system is part of the subtle bodies of the Earth and it both interpenetrates and surrounds the physical Earth.

The energy channels which make up this system form a three dimensional matrix which is present everywhere (on land, sea, and air) and which passes through all things on the Earth, including living beings. Ley lines (which are straight lines connecting sacred sites) are sometimes, but not always, near major energy channels. The Earth's gridwork system receives, stores, transforms, and transmits subtle energy. The gridwork system has three primary functions. First, it connects all living beings to the Earth. Second, it connects all living beings to each other. Third, it receives subtle energies from humans and from spiritual beings—both beings here on the Earth and non-terrestrial beings.

Sending energies to the Earth is a way that unseen spiritual beings can help humanity and at the same time fulfill their obligation to respect our free will and not be overly intrusive. These energies combine with the energies that are naturally present on our planet, both complementing them and increasing their effect.

Many people have noticed an acceleration in their personal or spiritual evolution after experiencing the energies of a sacred site, for example those at Stonehenge, England or in Sedona, Arizona, in the United States. What they are experiencing is a quicker, more concentrated form of a process which is happening to everyone on our planet simply by being in the presence of the subtle energies emitted by rocks and plants. The unseen spiritual beings who are helping humanity have been sending energies to the rocks, plants, and water of the

Earth throughout history; and now that the process is shifting into a higher gear. We are receiving more energies, stronger energies, and the energies are coming in at a faster rate. This is why so many people have the feeling that our evolution is speeding up.

When we understand the interconnections made by the Earth's gridwork system, it is easier to understand the interdependence of the Earth's evolutionary process and humanity's evolutionary process. If the Earth's gridwork increases in vibrational rate or if unseen spiritual beings enrich the gridwork with a new energy, then humans and all other living beings on the Earth are positively affected. When you receive an initiation your vibrational rate goes up because your subtle bodies are enriched by the presence of a new frequency. This transformation in you spreads out through the Earth's gridwork system and will have some positive effect on her and on all the living beings which inhabit her. Of course, the amount of this effect will depend on the type of initiation. While the direct effects of the energy initiations from the stars contained in this book are just on human beings, the initiations do have an indirect and positive effect on the Earth. Once you receive any of the initiations in this book, you will emit subtle energy frequencies which are helpful not only to yourself and others, but somewhat to Mother Earth's gridwork system and energy centers, especially her heart chakra. This will happen just by your being alive and won't require any conscious effort on your part!

Just as a human being has seven primary chakras, so too does Mother Earth. In a way similar to the major function of our human heart chakra—which is to help harmonize, balance, and develop our other chakras—the Earth's heart chakra functions to help harmonize, balance, and develop the Earth's other chakras. The Earth's heart chakra not only works with her own chakras' energies but encourages an attitude of tolerance between different peoples, thus promoting world peace. The Earth's heart chakra is located at Shambhala, in the Northern Gobi desert. Stonehenge, which is sometimes mentioned as the Earth's heart chakra, is actually located near the Earth's hara center. In humans the hara center is located about two to three finger widths below the navel and between one to two inches inside the body; it is an important center for the distribution of energy throughout the body. Similarly the Earth's hara center is an important center for the distribution of energy throughout the Earth's subtle body gridwork system. (We will expand this important discussion concerning the Earth's ˙ gridwork system and her heart chakra in the chapter on the Arcturus initiation and at other places later on in our journey.)

Now I want to clarify that we won't go into much detail about the technical intricacies and mechanics of the initiation process because our focus is on the broader understanding of initiation and its implications in daily life. I want to emphasize that it is not even necessary for you to understand the mechanics of this process to benefit from initiation, any more than you need to understand electrical theory to benefit from turning on a light. But let me lead into our next chapter on initiation with this brief comment about the value of the energies received during the initiation process. *A subtle energy initiation results in a permanent transformation in the invisible but very real energy fields that surround and interpenetrate your physical body.* It enriches these fields by adding to them one or more frequencies of subtle energy that were not previously present. In some cases it is a higher vibrational frequency; in other cases it is simply a different frequency, thereby facilitating a qualitative change in our way of being in the world. These initiations, or energy blessings from the stars, are an exciting and valuable energy experience offered by the spiritual masters to those people interested in growth and service.

Chapter 4

INITIATION

Conversation between Virginia and Irving

VE: Now that we've clarified what energy is and what it does, let's discuss how it's applied in the initiation process. What would you like to say about initiation?

IF: The word "initiation" comes from a Latin word that means, "to begin." A true initiation is a new beginning, a moving into a new way of being. An analogy that has often been used is that it is stepping through a doorway. This is an analogy that the Tibetan master D.K. often uses in the Alice Bailey writings.

Everyday life is filled with various initiations, such as graduation from high school or college, getting married, joining a service club or other special organization such as the Lions, Kiwanis, Elks, Odd Fellows, etc. There are also many religious initiations such as baptisms, bar mitzvahs, etc. However, the initiations that this book describes are examples of a particular kind of initiation, namely spiritual initiation.

Now, there are two ways that we can look at or define a spiritual initiation—in terms of its *meaning* or in terms of its underlying *mechanics*. If we look at the inner meaning of an initiation, a good way to define it is as a process that, to use D.K.'s phrase, makes us "more aware of ourselves as an embodied soul." The initiation may increase this awareness directly or it may help this awareness evolve thorough facilitating some trait, such as the ability to experience unconditional love. If we look at initiation in terms of the mechanics, a good definition is the one that D.K. uses several times in the Alice Bailey writings, where he refers to the process of initiation as *"a progressive sequence of directed energy impacts."*

From the esoteric point of view, *initiation involves a permanent transformation in your subtle body energy fields.* It is important to understand that initiation is not about intellectual learning; it is a permanent change in your very structure and therefore your being. In the esoteric worldview, each of us is surrounded by a nested sequence of energy fields. Although most people are unaware of these fields, they are very real and their condition has a profound effect on our consciousness and our way of being in the world—the way that we think, act, and feel in relationship to ourselves, our environment, and to other people. We know from daily life that even simple changes in our energy can produce significant changes in our thoughts and feelings. For example, if we are depressed we can listen to music, exercise, or open a window to let in more oxygen. The purpose of initiation is to produce a permanent transformation in your energy field that produces a transformation in your way of being in the world.

VE: Is initiation a specialized topic of interest just to a few people, or does initiation occupy a greater place in the grand scheme of things?

IF: Initiation is a topic of interest to anyone sincerely pursuing personal or spiritual growth. Initiation is at the very heart of how the universe is structured. To understand this, one first has to appreciate a basic fact about spiritual evolution, which is that it is endless. Certain milestones along the spiritual path have come to be labeled with words like "enlightenment." There is a danger in using a word like enlightenment because it implies that there is a final resting-place, an end point. There is no end point. One way to see this is to realize that no matter how far along the path you've gone there is a gap between you and God. Mystical traditions teach us that we are manifestations of God, but we are not equal with God. So, no matter how far you've gone, there is further that you can go in manifesting such divine attributes as love, compassion, and wisdom.

Once one realizes that spiritual evolution is endless, it becomes clear that everyone can gain by receiving initiations from beings who are further along the path than they are. For example, one of my many teachers is the Tibetan master, D.K. In the Alice Bailey channeled writings, he talks about his relationship with his teacher, Kuthumi, from whom he received teachings and initiations. Now, D.K. is still receiving teachings and initiations from Kuthumi, and Kuthumi is receiving teachings and initiations from his teacher, and on and on. This great chain of initiations ultimately stretches all the way back to God, the only being in the universe who doesn't stand to benefit from initiation.

Not only are we humans receiving initiations, but the Earth too is receiving initiations. The Earth's initiations interlock with the initiations which humanity is receiving. And both these sets of initiations (those of the Earth and those of humanity) are linked with initiations that our Sun is receiving. Initiations the Sun is receiving are linked to initiations that other stars are receiving. The entire universe can be seen as a giant network of inter-linked initiation systems. The vastness and grandeur of this network is equaled only by its beauty.

I don't mean to imply that it is essential for everyone to receive initiations. You can evolve spiritually working totally on your own. But we're all in this game together. None of us exists alone. This is the great lesson that love has to teach us. It's not that you can't do it without help, but rather that it takes so much longer. Doing it without help is like reinventing the wheel.

VE: You gave examples of receiving initiations from non-physical teachers; I assume you also include the possibility of initiations from physical Earth teachers such as gurus.

IF: Definitely! The reason I gave the examples I did is to emphasize that even the non-physical masters themselves are receiving initiations. In fact, there are some initiations— for example, certain grounding initiations—which must be received from physical teachers because the vibrations of non-physical masters are too high. Some initiations must be received from physical beings, some must be received from non-physical beings, and some can be received from either.

VE: You mentioned that initiation is of interest to anyone pursuing personal or spiritual growth. Can you say more about that?

IF: First I want to emphasize that initiations are not a substitute for continuing to work on one's personal or spiritual growth. However, initiations can dramatically accelerate that growth. I base my conclusion on personal observation of the many people with whom I have worked. It is also the conclusion reached by many religious traditions that have been giving energy initiations for thousands of years. The reason energy initiations can so effectively accelerate growth is that they permanently impart to the receiver a shakti—that is a non-physical energy that behaves intelligently. All the benefits conferred by spiritual initiation come through shakti.

I encourage anyone interested in personal or spiritual growth to seriously consider making a choice to do the initiations in this book—and more generally to look at the choices they have made about receiving energy. As you mentioned in the opening chapter, everyone, whether they realize it or not, has made one or more of four possible choices about receiving energy. The first essential choice is to consciously accept or refuse receiving energy from any outside source.

A second choice recognizes that there is a source greater than yourself, an infinite reservoir of general spiritual energies that are available to anybody at any time regardless of their sex, age, race, color, culture, or creed. These energies can be received whenever a prayer or request is made to a particular spiritual being, (for example Jesus, Mother Mary, Buddha, or your guardian angel) or they can be invoked by appeal to God, Light, Truth, Source, and so on. These "public domain" energies insure that any call for help will be answered. The only prerequisite is a willingness to ask and receive.

A third choice is to receive a lineage initiation from a person in a physical body, such as an Eastern guru. A lineage is a group of beings entrusted with the responsibility of transmitting initiations that are particularly important or require accompanying information to be safely received or effectively used. A lineage initiation must be received from an official representative of the appropriate lineage. It also requires some level of conscious awareness on the part of the recipient about the significance of the initiation, of how to benefit from it or use it.

A fourth choice is to receive an energy lineage initiation from a non-physical master such as those associated with the seven different stars systems in this book. The decision to make this fourth choice, possibly in addition to the second and/or third choice, can be one of the most useful and beautiful decisions a person can make.

VE: Now that we've reviewed those four initiation choices once more, I'd like to move on to the particular initiations in this book. Can you give us an overview of the purpose and structure of these initiations?

IF: The initiations in this book come from non-terrestrial spiritual masters associated with seven different star systems. However, two preparatory initiations must first be done in order to receive the seven star initiations. The primary purpose of all nine initiations is to develop and amplify universal love or what some call Christ Consciousness. I wish to emphasize that one does not have to be a Christian to be interested in Christ Consciousness, for the hallmark of this higher state of consciousness is unconditional love for all beings. We use the term Christ (which literally means "the anointed" in Greek) as a title applicable to many beings, not just as a reference to Jesus. We use Christ Consciousness as a useful label for a higher state known to many traditions throughout history; we ask everyone to interpret this term in the broadest, most universal manner. The reasons the initiations in this book are coming to the planet now is that humanity has evolved to a point of readiness.

The initiations are meant to function together as a system. Nonetheless, the spiritual masters who designed this system did it so ingeniously that anyone can receive as many or as few of the star initiations as desired and can do the initiations in any order after receiving the two preparatory initiations. The optimal approach, of course, is to do all of the initiations and to specifically do them in the order given in the book.

VE: You've touched on several important themes that we can return to as we discuss each of the star initiations. For now, I would like to focus on your statement that the initiations in this book come from non-terrestrial masters. Some people will find the idea of receiving energies from non-terrestrial sources to be nearly unbelievable. What would you say to them?

IF: First of all, it's not at all odd to think that there is intelligent life elsewhere in the universe. It's been jokingly said that if the Earth is the only place where there's intelligent life, then there's an awful lot of wasted space in the universe. Looking at it more scientifically, many astronomers now believe that there is intelligent life throughout the cosmos. Doesn't it also make sense that intelligent beings on other worlds would evolve spiritual traditions? And doesn't a part of being truly spiritual include the desire to help others?

We also know that spiritual evolution brings with it the development of certain paranormal powers, including telepathy. Because of the great masters' highly developed telepathic powers, transmissions can easily occur regardless of the distance between the sender and the receiver. Putting all these facts together is it really that difficult to imagine a network of spiritual masters on different planets who work together to facilitate the evolution of those who are not as far along the path than they are?

To the person who is still skeptical, I would ask only that they remain open to the possibility that something with which they are not familiar could still be true. They may well be surprised at what happens.

VE: Some people might be concerned about any dangers or discomforts that the initiations could bring. Would you say more about that?

IF: Readers of this book will receive the initiations directly from beings who are often referred to by the term Ascended Masters. It is difficult for us to even imagine the high level of love and wisdom such beings have attained. Any initiation from such a compassionate and advanced being will always intend your highest spiritual good. However, any initiation begins a process of inner growth and clearing and will likely cause some discomfort.

It is very important to understand that if you pursue any path, whether it is energy work or something else that is genuinely and deeply transformational, then eventually you could experience some discomfort. This is true at any level of your being—physically, emotionally, or mentally. Physically, you might experience intense heat or tingling as energy channels that have been relatively closed begin to open up. This is similar to being out of shape, going to the gym to start working out, and getting sore muscles. On the emotional level, if you pursue personal growth long enough you will realize things about yourself that you wish weren't so, and you could have painful, repressed emotions come up. Energy work can even bring up emotions around issues you thought you had completely resolved. If that happens, it means that the energy is working on deeper levels of the issue that are still there. On a mental level, it can be difficult to give up cherished beliefs, even when we realize that they are incorrect. Mentally, the energies can cause us to see ourselves or other people or the world in different ways, and that can be uncomfortable.

The initiations in this book are truly transformational. They are not for people who are just enchanted with the idea of transformation, but for responsible people open to change who want actual, deep transformation.

VE: Irving, you and I both know that transformation at this deep level can be extremely challenging, and that even though the discomfort is only temporary—and it's all for a good purpose—it can feel downright unpleasant. What suggestions do you have so that people can help themselves through this process since we are not responsible for their experience and aren't offering medical advice?

IF: To be sure, it is very important to use common sense. So create a sacred time and quiet space every day. Get good nutrition, plenty of sleep, and don't push yourself too hard. Some people may find that body work, emotional support, and other healing processes could be useful.

Additionally, you will be supported through all of the initiations in this book by use of a special energy technology developed by a master who goes by the initials T.K. (that's T, not D as in Djwhal). Of the many masters behind the S.U.N. organization, T.K. is the one with whom I work most often. He is an absolute stickler for making energies safe and for reducing the amount of discomfort they can cause. All of the initiations that S.U.N. gives, and all of the initiations in this book, make use of this new energy technology T.K. has developed called "star tetrahedron technology." It is important to understand that subtle energy, like physical energy, obeys certain laws. Therefore, there is a science and a technology to energy initiations, and much progress is being made to help humans by increasing both the transformative power of initiations and the ease with which people can receive them.

Through the unique way it makes use of the naturally occurring star tetrahedron shapes in the human energy field, T.K.'s star tetrahedron technology makes it possible for energies to be integrated more deeply into a human being's subtle energy fields. A star tetrahedron is a three-dimensional representation of a Star of David. It can be formed by combining two intersecting tetrahedra, one pointing up and one pointing down. A tetrahedron is a pyramid shape, in which each of the four faces is an equilateral triangle; it's not an Egyptian style pyramid with a square base. T.K.'s new technology also makes it easier for a shakti to constantly measure all of a person's major energy centers and pathways so as to reduce discomfort to the lowest level possible. Painful emotions or thoughts that might otherwise take months to process can take only weeks with an initiation based on star tetrahedron technology.

Even with all of the above considerations, of course, each person will have to decide for himself or herself whether to take the initiations described in this book. Some people may wish to ask Jesus, Buddha, Mother Mary, an angel, or some other spiritual figure to whom they are attracted, to oversee the initiations for them.

Before doing the initiations, then, each person needs to be totally convinced, by whatever means are individually appropriate, that the initiations are safe and for his or her highest good. I want to make it very clear that no one is being pressured to do these initiations. Also, although people who experience the transformative power of these initiations will naturally want to share them with friends, I request that no one pressure anyone else into doing the initiations.

VE: Some people might believe they are not yet ready to receive these initiations because they feel unworthy. They might feel their subtle bodies are in need of healing, strengthening, or clearing before they can proceed. What would you say to them?

IF: Everyone is worthy of receiving the initiations because it is the birthright of each human to experience Christ Consciousness. *These initiations are a universal dispensation for all humanity.* Any necessary preparation of the subtle bodies is done by the two preliminary initiations. Feeling that one is not ready to start even the preliminary initiations would be like feeling one cannot start cleaning one's house because it is dirty. It is the very job of these preliminary initiations to strengthen, clear, and otherwise prepare the subtle bodies to better incorporate the seven energy blessings that follow.

VE: Then let's go on to describe these two preparatory initiations and explain how one can best receive them.

PREPARATORY INITIATIONS

IF: First, I want to emphasize that it is absolutely necessary for anyone who wants to do any of the seven star initiations to *first receive both of the two preparatory initiations in the* *exact order given in the book.*

The first preparatory initiation is the *Subtle Body Fortification Attunement* which strengthens the subtle bodies and also does some clearing. The reason this initiation is essential is that the star energy initiations use very powerful frequencies that have not been released to the Earth previously. Therefore, it is necessary for the subtle bodies to be built up so that they can hold and safely conduct these frequencies. Even if you have previously done energy work, even if you have done advanced energy work, and even if you are a professional teacher of energy work, you still need to receive both the *Subtle Body Fortification Attunement* and the *Anti-Glamour Initiation*!

When someone is ready to receive the *Subtle Body Fortification Attunement*, all they have to do is ask the masters associated with the seven different star systems to collectively send the initiation. While there are no required rituals or symbols, three steps are recommended to help you focus your intention:

1. Go into your quiet inner space of peace.
2. Verify that your heart and mind are really willing to receive the initiation.
3. Make a request such as, "I request the masters to send me the *Subtle Body Fortification Attunement*."

Your sincere desire and request to receive the initiation will automatically result in your receiving it. The initiation, like each initiation in the book, takes roughly an hour and a quarter to be transmitted to your subtle body fields. The shakti of each initiation then continues to be present with you from that point forward. You may well acquire a deeper experience from each initiation process by remaining in your quiet inner space the entire hour and a quarter. However, it is okay to receive the initiation while doing something else—as long as the possibility of your being distracted by the initiation does not raise any safety issues for yourself or others. *Once you have received the Subtle Body Fortification Attunement, or any other initiation, you need to wait at least a week before going on to the next initiation.*

The other preparatory initiation, which must be done after the *Subtle Body Fortification Attunement* and before any of the other seven star energy initiations, is the *Anti-Glamour Initiation.*

VE: Just so there's no confusion about the spiritual meaning of the word glamour, could you define it and say more about this *Anti-Glamour Initiation,* please?

IF: Glamour is illusion. When we succumb to glamour we are like a desert traveler who believes that a mirage is real. An example of glamour is the glamour of money. Now I want to draw a distinction between the glamour of money and money itself. I'm not saying there is anything inherently wrong with money. The problem is the *glamour* of money—the belief that by having enough money we can guarantee our happiness or escape the adversities of life. This is an illusion. The truth is that people who have a great deal of money are not necessarily any happier than those who don't have much money. Not only have the great spiritual teachers been telling us this for ages, there are now multiple scientific studies that show there is little correlation between being wealthy and being happy.

A person with an interest in spiritual development often recognizes the glamours that exist in mainstream society—glamours associated with money, fame, possessions, power, and control over others. These are all things that shift our focus to the external world and away from the realization that the ultimate source of happiness is in our own heart and comes from union with the Divine. Even some spiritually-oriented people don't recognize that many of the preoccupations common to the New Age movement are simply analogs of the glamours that we see in mainstream society. These preoccupations create the illusion that our salvation lies in some person or event in the external world that does not require our own growth and change. One example is the belief that a profound planetary energy shift will occur on such and such a date and will be the salvation of humanity. (Oh yes, and then there are the UFO lift-off stories.) Energy shifts do occur, and they can be important. But they are the soil in which we must grow the fruit of our own salvation which only happens through hard work on an individual level.

People who do energy work often succumb to the glamour that if only they can receive enough initiations they will automatically become enlightened. Energy work facilitates the development of higher states of consciousness, but no amount of energy work by itself can guarantee that an individual is going to become enlightened. The great spiritual traditions emphasize that energy work is secondary in importance to the hard work of traditional or classical meditation—not contemporary practices, such as guided imagery and creative visualizations, which have been inaccurately labeled as meditation.

With respect to the initiations in this book, there are two glamours to which a person might be particularly likely to succumb. One of them is the belief that just because an energy is coming from a non-terrestrial source it is somehow inherently better than the energies that one can access here on Earth. Another is the belief that someone who has received these star initiations is somehow better than someone who hasn't. D.K. tells us in the Alice Bailey writings that a master is not superior to an earthworm, for both are equally manifestations of God.

There are many, many glamours. The Tibetan master D.K. wrote a book through Alice Bailey called <u>Glamour: A World Problem</u>—a wonderful book for helping us to understand how insidious and widespread glamour is. The subtitle of the book indicates the magnitude of the problem, yet very few people in the New Age movement even discuss glamour. One of the reasons that the Spiritual Hierarchy is willing to allow this book, <u>Energy Blessings from the Stars</u>, to be published—since it introduces an initiatory energy system of such great magnitude—is that the seven star initiations require the *Anti-Glamour Initiation.*

VE: Good. So how does one receive the *Anti-Glamour Initiation?* And how do its effects compare to the effects of the

Subtle Body Fortification Attunement?

IF: The directions for receiving the *Anti-Glamour Initiation* are the same in all respects as those for receiving the *Subtle Body Fortification Attunement*. There are no required rituals or symbols, but we definitely recommend the same three-step procedure described previously. First, go into your inner space. Second, verify that your mind and heart are willing to receive the initiation. Third, express your desire to receive the initiation. For example, you could say, "I now request the masters of all seven star systems to collectively send the *Anti-Glamour Initiation*." Remember that after receiving the *Anti-Glamour Initiation* for one hour and 15 minutes, you need to wait at least one week before starting the next initiation.

One difference in the effect of the two preparatory initiations is that by the end of the week-long *Subtle Body Fortification Attunement* the energy will have finished building up the subtle bodies to the degree necessary. However, the shakti of the *Anti-Glamour Initiation* will continue to work with you to reveal your glamours and to help you release them *for the rest of your life*. Recognition and release of glamour is definitely an ongoing process!

Once you have done both of these two preparatory initiations, you can then do as many or as few of the star initiations as you choose, and you can do them in any order you prefer. However, the optimal approach is definitely to do all of them and to do them in the order given in the book.

Please remember that it is necessary to wait at least one week between any two initiations. However, some people might prefer to wait longer. For those particularly sensitive to energy, it might take them a while to feel comfortable with the level of energy that is being transmitted for them. Other people might want to wait longer simply because they are really enjoying the process. Also, people might have many interesting insights about themselves and feel they want to take time to process them. Some people might want to keep a notebook of such insights and/or record the experiences they have while receiving the various initiations. This can be particularly useful for people who aren't that sensitive to subtle energy, as it can help them see that the initiations are bringing about very real changes.

VE: In addition to the ones you've just mentioned what other experiences might a person expect from receiving the initiations?

IF: First I want to emphasize that the subjective experience of the same initiation can be quite different for different people. Speaking very generally, an initiation associated with a particular trait can result either in immediately experiencing that trait more strongly or in first experiencing the surfacing of blocks to that trait. For example, the Arcturian initiation, which is the first of the star initiations, is associated with hope. All those receiving the Arcturian initiation will eventually feel more hopeful than ever before. However, some people may first experience the surfacing of feelings—such as distrust or pessimism—that have been blocking their experience of hope. Those receiving the initiations may have unusually vivid dreams or unusually deep meditations, childhood or past life memories, temporary mood swings and so forth. People who are sensitive to their chakras will probably notice a lot of activity in them.

VE: Could you briefly describe the chakras to which you just referred?

IF: *The chakras are subtle body centers for the receipt, storage, transformation and distribution of energy.* Traditionally they are seven in number and are connected to the physical body in certain designated areas. Each chakra is associated with characteristic patterns of thinking, feeling and acting.

A chakra is a spinning vortex of subtle matter. It has both a front and a back; so, seen clairvoyantly, there is one cone or funnel shape widening out as we move away from a person's front and another cone or funnel shape (interconnecting with the first one) widening out as we move away from a person's back. If you look at a chakra more closely, you can see that it has parts, traditionally labeled "petals", because they look like the petals of a flower and, like a flower's petals, they are structured in layers. In fact, a good way to visualize a chakra is as a spinning flower. **(See Illustration #2)**

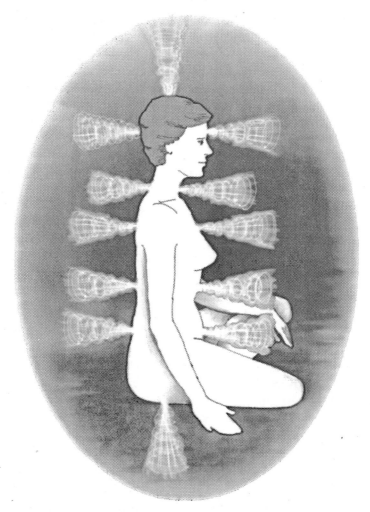

Illustration #2 - The chakras are subtle body centers for the receipt, storage, transformation, and distribution of energy. A chakra is a spinning vortex of subtle matter that connects to the physical body in both the front and the back. Traditionally there are seven primary chakras.

In addition to feeling energy in the seven traditional chakras, people who are sensitive to the chakras above the head and below the feet may feel energy there—and some people may become aware of these centers for the first time. I am referring to a sequence of centers, spaced roughly six inches apart, which some refer to as "out of the body chakras" and which lie above the head and also to a corresponding sequence of centers which lie below the feet. The two most important of these for energy work are the soul star, located about six to eight inches above the head, and a dual center called the earth star, located about six to eight inches below the feet. The soul star modulates energies that are coming into our field from the cosmos; the earth star modulates energies that are coming into our field from the Earth. By "modulates" I refer to changing the frequency and/or amplitude of the energy. It's important again to understand that all energy, including subtle energy, has both a frequency and amplitude. Just as food that we take in is broken down and recombined, energy that we take in from the environment is modulated and combined with other energies.

The reason that the soul star has its name is that it is the primary energy center through which the soul and the Solar Angel send energy to us. The soul and the Solar Angel could send energy to any part of your subtle bodies but their transmissions are more effective if they first pass the energy through the soul star, because of its capacity to modulate energy. Because the soul star is always filled with the energy of the soul and the Solar Angel, it is used in some key esoteric practices for accelerating spiritual evolution. I should say that I don't recommend to anyone that they try to place the energies of the initiations described in this book in their soul star or in their earth star. This will happen anyway. It's included as part of the initiation and it's part of the divine intelligence of the energy. By trying to fiddle with it you can't improve the situation, you can only decrease the effectiveness of the initiation.

VE: Do you have any final advice for people on how to go about receiving these two preparatory and the other seven star initiations?

IF: These initiations are meant for everyone in the world—people of all spiritual backgrounds, people who have no spiritual background, even people who are totally skeptical. That's why there's not a specific ritual or form associated with any of the initiations. However, people should feel free to associate any initiation with whatever helps them to feel more open and comfortable—a ritual, an appeal to a particular spiritual being, music, nature, and so on.

I want to emphasize again that the energy in these initiations is divine energy and that the initiations do not contain anyone's personal energy—including Virginia, myself, and even the masters who will be sending you the initiations. I also want to emphasize that no one should receive these initiations until they are completely convinced in both mind and heart that the initiations are in their highest good. Once someone has asked to receive the initiations, they need to accept the responsibility for the experiences that they have.

In doing the initiations be as free as possible from preconceptions about what they will be like. Above all, be open to the possibility that they will help you to transform beyond what you believed was possible. Although each person receiving an initiation has their own unique experiences, perhaps **Illustration #3** (next page) can suggest those possibilities.

Illustration #3 - Energy from a star initiation can assume many geometrical forms as it flows into the subtle bodies. This illustration shows just one phase of one initiation.

You must have completed the *Subtle Body Fortification Attunement* and the *Anti-Glamour Initiation* (see pages 69-74) prior to taking any of the seven star initiations. You may now proceed with Arcturus or any of the seven star initiations using the process described below.

How to Receive the Seven Star Initiations

1. After doing the *Subtle Body Fortification Attunement* and *Anti-Glamour Initiation*, in that order, you can do as few or as many of the **star energy initiations** as you want, and you can do them in any order. However, you will definitely get the most benefit if you do all seven star energy initiations and do them in the order given in the book.

2. Each star energy initiation takes approximately one hour and 15 minutes to be received. Each initiation only needs to be done *once in your lifetime*.

3. You must wait at least one full week between receiving any of the nine initiations (*Subtle Body Fortification Attunement, Anti-Glamour Initiation*, and the seven star energy initiations).

4. To receive any of the star initiations, ask the spiritual masters associated with that star to send you the initiation in this manner. Go into your quiet inner space. Verify that your mind and heart are ready to receive the initiation. Make a statement such as, "I request the masters of _____(for example, Arcturus) to send me the initiation for ____(for example, hope). Do not do this process while driving or while engaging in other activities where distraction could create a safety issue!

5. The initiations can be received either individually or in groups of two or more. You are encouraged to share the processes in this book with one or more friends. However, please do not pressure anyone into receiving the initiations.

6. Receiving any star energy initiation does not empower you to initiate others.

Chapter 5

ARCTURUS – THE BLESSING OF HOPE

Commentary by Irving

Before receiving this or any of the other star initiations, it is necessary to receive the *Subtle Body Fortification Attunement* and *Anti-Glamour Initiation* as explained on pages 69-74. Like the other star initiations, you can receive this Arcturian initiation simply by asking for it (after doing the *Subtle Body Fortification Attunement* and *Anti-Glamour Initiation*). It is recommended that you **read this chapter** before asking for and receiving this initiation. Like the other star initiations, it takes about an hour and a quarter to receive the entire initiation. Please refer to page 79 to review the star initiation process.

This initiation comes from the Arcturian masters who hold the energies of divine love in a joyful way and are therefore adept at gifting humanity with the qualities of hope and joy. Indeed, in Hawaii Arcturus is known as Hoku-lea, "the star of gladness." Hope is essentially lightness of heart combined with faith in the inherent goodness of life. Although hope may manifest as hope about a particular situation, the quality we are talking about is the transcendent hope which arises spontaneously without dependence on the external environment. It is both deeper and more significant than hope about one particular situation. Hope is characterized by the free flow of energy in the etheric body; lightness, expansion and flexibility in the emotional body; stability and openness in the mental body.

With sufficient spiritual development everyone manifests this quality of hope, just as everyone ultimately manifests unconditional love. Hope is important for the individual and for humanity for two primary reasons: 1) Energized by hope we can accomplish things which we otherwise could not. 2) Hope has a profound clearing effect on the subtle bodies, particularly the mental body, thereby speeding up our ability to absorb higher level spiritual frequencies. Hope also enlivens the lungs, oxygenates the body, and increases our ability to absorb energy.

In both mainstream and New Age society there are many different negative thought forms about the future of the Earth and of humanity. The truth is that the future of humanity is increasingly bright! It is therefore essential for anyone on a serious spiritual path not to succumb to these negative thought forms as they will impede his or her progress. Many people are actually addicted to these thought forms because they are afraid to feel hope or to experience the clearing of the subtle bodies that hope brings.

Hope is one of the most treasured of our natural birthrights. The French author Victor Hugo referred to it as, "the word which God has written on the brow of every man." In I Corinthians in the New Testament, hope is considered one of the three primary traits of Christian character. One of the most beautiful stories about hope is the Greek myth of Pandora's box. When the box was opened, a swarm of all the miseries that afflict humanity escaped, so that nothing remained but hope.

This initiation comes from a group of Arcturian masters who wish to assist humanity. Arcturus is a giant yellow star about 20-25 times the size of our Sun, and is the brightest star in the constellation of Boötes (pronounced: bo-'oh-teez), located approximately thirty-five light-years from Earth. Arcturus is the fourth brightest star in the heavens and can be found by following the sweep of the Big Dipper's handle as it moves away from the bowl of the Dipper.

The Arcturians have been facilitating the co-evolution

of planet Earth and the human species ever since cellular life first appeared on our planet. They are one of the three groups helping the most with the evolution of our planetary gridwork system, the other two helpers being the Sirians and the Pleideians. One specialty of the Arcturians is facilitating the functioning and evolution of the Earth's heart chakra. Favorite focal points for the Arcturian energy include mountains and rock structures, such as the Great Pyramid of Giza in Egypt and Stonehenge in England, which serve to ground frequencies from the Earth's heart chakra to stabilize the Earth's gridwork system.

Edgar Cayce remarked that Arcturus is one of the most advanced civilizations in our entire galaxy. Indeed, its importance has been recognized since ancient times. In ancient Lemuria, Arcturian energies were used primarily in the development of what has been called "female Christ Consciousness," and the Lemurians produced a number of significant feminine Christ figures.

Until now the most significant star for the development of Christ Consciousness has been Sirius. (For more about this see the chapter on Sirius.) However, over the next thousand years the most important star influencing the development of Christ Consciousness will be Arcturus.

Latent within the human heart are seven energy structures called "Christ Seeds," all of which must be completely activated before Christ Consciousness can fully manifest in an individual. (Each of these seeds is associated with one of the seven primary attributes of Christ Consciousness, which will be described more fully in the Sirian chapter.) Humanity's primary guides in activating these seeds will be the Arcturians. However, activation of the Christ Seeds is something which will take place for humanity as a whole sometime in the future. At the present time, the primary focus of the Arcturians is to assist in a general way with development of the human heart, the heart chakra, and the emotional body.

Arcturian energies contain a significant amount of the metaphysical water element. For this reason, although

Arcturian energies are associated with developing both the yin and yang aspects of Christ Consciousness, they are associated more with the yin aspects. Arcturian energies help to integrate the conscious and unconscious mind, facilitate dreamwork, and combine well with the energies of the Moon. On a physical level the Arcturians are facilitating and accelerating our material evolutionary process by helping the water in our cells become even more structured. It is important to realize that the water in living cells is not like tap water. It is so highly structured that some have referred to it as a liquid crystal. Like a crystal, structured water can contain much energy and information. Let me repeat the fact that it is a natural part of spiritual evolution for the water in the human cells to become ever and ever more structured.

Conversation between Virginia and Irving

VE: Thank you for your information about Arcturus in the constellation of Boötes. I was interested in the fact that Arcturus is about 36 light-years from us compared to the Sirians who are only 8.6 and the Pleiadians who are roughly 400 light-years away. So it seems the Sirian influence has been physically closer. You said that the Arcturian influence has been here since cellular life appeared on the Earth. Does this imply they were here before the Pleiadians but after the Sirians, or does physical distance matter?

IF: Well, actually Sirius, the Pleiades, and Arcturus are all important stars for humanity, and they've all been working with us, often as a trio, from the very beginning. They've all been helping the evolution of both humanity and the planet Earth—and that evolution has involved both the physical plane and the subtle body planes.

VE: Does the fact that the Arcturians are so associated with love mean they have a special relationship to the Earth's heart chakra?

IF: Yes. The Arcturians are particularly adept at working with the Earth's heart chakra, both in a general way and in order to ground Christ energies. In general, when I talk about grounding, I mean the movement of energy from a less dense plane to a more dense plane. Through the Alice Bailey writings, the Tibetan master D.K. has told us that there is an extraordinarily important relationship between the Earth's heart chakra and the heart chakra of the Sun; indeed, it is only through that sustained relationship that humanity is able to reach higher stages of spiritual evolution. I have received additional information that there is an extremely important energy triangle involving the heart chakra of the Earth, the heart chakra of the Sun, and the heart chakra of Arcturus. This triangle acts to ground Christ energies as well as other spiritual energies coming into the Earth by directing a flow of these energies into the Earth's base chakra. Its action for the Earth is similar to the action of the pineal gland in the human body, for one of the primary functions of the pineal gland is to ground and integrate spiritual energies throughout the human body.

VE: In addition to helping us as individuals to develop Christ Consciousness, do the Arcturian and the other six initiations described in this book help with the development of Christ Consciousness on a planetary scale?

IF: Definitely, although indirectly. Anybody who receives even one of the initiations in this book will help to ground into the Earth's heart chakra the energies that are coming into the planet. The more initiations they receive, the more they will help. This happens automatically without any extra effort because each of the initiations in this book incorporates a different key frequency or frequencies from the Earth's heart chakra. Because the Arcturians are particularly adept at working with the Earth's heart chakra, the initiation in this chapter is especially useful in helping people facilitate the grounding of Christ energies.

VE: Do the Arcturians have names we should know, or is there anything specific that would help us to have a sense of identity with them as a consciousness?

IF: That's a good question. Actually what they and the other masters have told me is that they prefer to remain anonymous. They prefer to keep the emphasis on the process of inner work and how the energies can facilitate that process. One of the signs of true spiritual teachers is that they emphasize the message and not themselves, the messenger. The masters from Arcturus and the other six star systems are at a level where they're merging their consciousness for the group good.

VE: Now here is a question that interests me. My understanding is that the Arcturians are working with us in two ways—some are physically present in space craft and some are working from a distance telepathically. Can you comment on this?

IF: I'm open to the possibility that there are actually Arcturian spacecraft out there, but I've never seen one personally. The important thing to understand is that they do not need to be physically present to utilize their powers. These beings can do anything they need to do from Arcturus. There are beings on Earth—for example, certain gurus—who are so evolved that they can materialize and dematerialize matter. Since the beings we're talking about are even more evolved than that, they have the advantage of not needing to be here in physical form.

VE: In this book we have defined non-terrestrials specifically as those beings who are spiritually enlightened masters and, as you just indicated, do not have to be physically present on the Earth to utilize their powers. However, many people are concerned about what they call "extra-terrestrials" that are not so benevolent and are worried about UFOs being a sign of their physical presence here on the Earth. Do you have any comments about these matters?

IF: The subject of UFOs is certainly one where I don't claim to have all of the answers. I believe that the Earth has definitely been visited by extra-terrestrial spacecraft. I also believe that many of the reported sightings and encounters with UFOs have other explanations. It is an open question in my mind as to how often the Earth has been visited by such craft and what the purposes of these visits might be.

I do know one thing. Life is uncertain, and it is easy to let yourself be ruled by fears of anything—whether it's UFOs, being mugged, dying in a fire or earthquake, etc. The important thing is to live a life of love, not fear. And it is our spiritual practices which keep us growing in love. I would suggest that there are two questions which are much more important to ask yourself than the question, "Do I need to worry about UFOs?" Those more important questions are: "Am I showing love for myself, my fellow human beings, and Mother Earth?"; "Have I meditated today?" Through meditation you will not only grow spiritually, you will also develop the ability to receive answers to questions about UFOs and many other matters.

VE: So when we're talking about Arcturian masters being located many light-years away from Earth, we're really interpreting distance as a measure of limitation rather than understanding that instantaneous communication is the normal pattern for such evolved beings.

IF: Yes. I gave you the example of being able to materialize or dematerialize matter, but of course that's not the primary thing that these spiritual masters from other star systems are doing. The primary thing that the Arcturians and other masters are doing is telepathically communicating information and energy to us. It's important to understand the intimate relationship between telepathy and consciousness, which allows instantaneous transmission regardless of the distance between the sender and the receiver.

VE: So when we receive an initiation from Arcturus or other stars, how can that telepathic transmission of energy affect our physical bodies?

IF: What's being transmitted is subtle energy, and human beings have the inborn capacity to absorb subtle energy from the universe and incorporate it into our physical body. This process is analogous to how a plant can turn sunlight into nutrients.

VE: A part of our bodies that I feel is particularly important to understand is the blood. What are the metaphysical properties of the blood and what is the connection with Arcturus?

IF: To talk about the blood is particularly appropriate with respect to Arcturus. Let me explain—because some readers may not be familiar with this concept—that every organ, every gland, every part of your body has some metaphysical, esoteric function as well as a physical function. In some cases, the metaphysical or spiritual function is clear. For example, the brain on a metaphysical level is involved with thought while on a physical level it regulates the whole body. In some cases, it's not as obvious. For example, one of the many metaphysical and spiritual functions of the kidneys is to mediate compassion and kindness, or what some people have called loving kindness, the milk of kindness.

So the blood has very important metaphysical functions. Perhaps one way to look at this is in terms of the rays, the Seven Rays of Creation. These rays are the fundamental energies or "building blocks" out of which all other energies are made. Understanding the rays is a very powerful way of understanding the architecture of spiritual reality. As an analogy, if you understand the periodic table of the elements, it helps you to understand the structure of the physical world in a very profound way. If you understand the rays, it helps you to understand the metaphysical and spiritual world in a very profound way. Indeed, one way to look at evolution for both the individual level and at the level of humanity as a whole is as a shift in our ray structure. The entire world can be seen as a giant quilt made up of many different colors, and those colors correspond to the rays. The quilt is constantly shifting and changing colors. It changes a little bit at a time, but in a thousand years it looks very different. This shifting pattern of ray energy explains both physical and spiritual evolution as well as the interrelation of the two. One way to approach understanding the metaphysical and spiritual functions of a body part is to look at what rays that body part is primarily working with. (Readers can refer to Appendix A in the back of the book for a short explanation of the rays.)

Now let me say that the primary ray energy that the blood is emanating is the Second Ray, which is the Ray of

Love/Wisdom. Of the seven rays, this is the one most closely associated with Arcturus. Because of its Second Ray properties, one of the metaphysical/spiritual functions of the blood is to manifest love, ultimately unconditional love. This is also apparent from the association of the blood with the heart. The blood is also the primary mechanism for the union of love and will (ultimately unconditional love and complete surrender to divine will).

What is not as often appreciated is that the next most powerful ray emanation from the blood is the Fourth Ray which is the Ray of Harmony and Harmony Through Conflict. One of the functions of the blood is to harmonize the dualities within ourselves, such as harmonizing matter and spirit. This duality between matter and spirit is the primary duality in the universe.

VE: If we look at this relationship between matter and spirit in terms of everyday life, does that mean the spiritual planes determine everything that happens on a physical level?

IF: Although the higher spiritual planes affect physical evolution, it's important not to over-interpret. It's common in the New Age movement to interpret every physical thing as having some deeper spiritual significance, and this is simply not the case. Spirit extends the physical realm but does not violate the autonomy of the physical realm. The great Hindu saint, Sri Aurobindo, said "Heaven's touch fulfills our Earth, but cancels it not." It's important to realize that in the process of evolution there is a random element. In the physical world there is such a thing as chance. It's sometimes said that everything happens for a some deeper reason, that there are no accidents, but that is a simplification. What is true and what's important to understand is that there is a higher order of forces at work in the universe. However, physical chance is very easy to demonstrate. Just toss a coin up in the air. In the long run it will come down heads half the time and tails half the time, but there's no observable pattern, no one can predict which way it's going to come up on a particular toss. That's chance. If anyone believes the contrary, I challenge them to go to a casino and if they can really predict, they'll become a million-aire very quickly. God did not create a world in which chance applies only to coins, but built it into the very fabric of the universe along with various physical laws.

This presence of chance is the analog for the material world of what free will is for people. It particularly saddens me when I see responsible people believing they must assume blame for all their problems, even certain illnesses. We need to remember that even plants can become diseased. It's no wonder with all the self-blame and resulting depression that the Arcturians feel we can benefit from the gift of hope!

VE: I hear that, and it's most encouraging. Now I want to bring our discussion back to the Arcturians' help in trans-forming the water in our cells to become more structured. How does getting the water structured affect other things that are happening to our bodies and our lives? Many light-workers, especially, seem to be going through enormously challenging and sometimes painful situations.

IF: The answer to that would depend on the individual case. Much of the life stress that light-workers experience is caused by having to integrate the many higher frequencies coming into the planet. Increased structuring of cellular wa-ter can help us because it facilitates stabilization of our energy fields. That change in the structure in the water affects us on all levels, physical, emotional, mental, and spiritual. Just to give an example, on the physical level, it could have the effect of making you more resistant to viral infections. However, the most important results of this change in the structure of the water are on a spiritual level.

VE: Are these incoming frequencies to the planet also shifting DNA cellular identity as we know it?

IF: There certainly are shifts which are occurring in DNA, although most of those are occurring in the subtle body of the DNA at this point in time rather than the physical DNA. The primary thing that is happening to people who are more spiri-tually evolved and more spiritually open is that there is a tremendous amount of clearing that is going on. So there's kind of an irony here in that during this very wonderful initiatory period, people who are more open and who are more spiritually evolved are actually having a more difficult time than people who are insensitive to personal and spiritual growth.

VE: This seems to make people who are interested in self-improvement and self-growth in consciousness feel confused because they would assume that if they are getting more spiritual they ought to be very healthy and quite cleansed emotionally.

IF: It would be nice if that were the case. However, all one has to do is look at many famous spiritual teachers today and see the health problems which they also have. Just like most people, they also die of cancer and heart disease, etc. So one might ask, "Is it worthwhile?" Why go through all of this massive clearing if you're going to have some very real physical, emotional, and mental discomforts as a result of it? And the answer is that it is very much worth it!

One of the central points which all the great spiritual traditions have taught us is that it is really only through spiritual evolution that we can be truly fulfilled. It is only through spiritual evolution that we can become independent enough of the physical plane so that we're not controlled by it. And this happens as a result of a change in a state of consciousness. I mentioned that famous spiritual teachers die of the same physical problems that we do. For example, Ramakrishna, one of the greatest Hindu saints of our time, or of any time, died of cancer of the throat. The difference is that he died in a state of bliss, whereas someone else who had that same condition might die in a state of agony. More to the point, not only did he die in a state of bliss, but he lived his entire life in a state of bliss.

VE: You've said the Arcturian initiation first focuses on hope, which has this clearing effect on our mental body and particularly the lungs, oxygenating our bodies and helping us absorb energy. Why is it that the Arcturian civilization is capable of bringing hope to a more precise influence than some other star group can right now?

IF: First of all, each star has a characteristic overall quality that's associated with it. While a star has many, many different frequencies, nonetheless, there's an overall quality when those frequencies act together. While a star will affect different people in different ways, it will tend to have certain major affects on most people. One of the things that the energy of Arcturus is particularly good at is awakening hope and its associated emotions such as joy and gladness.

It's important to realize that these states of joy and gladness that we're talking about are our natural birthright. The negative thinking, pessimism, sadness, grief, etc., are really more superficial; our deeper birthright is to be joyful. When we're talking about hope and joy, we're talking about what might really be called transcendent hope and transcendent joy. These bear a relationship to ordinary joy and ordinary hope that is analogous to the relationship of unconditional love to ordinary love. It's a natural part of the process of spiritual evolution that these inherently joyful, hopeful qualities of the heart be unmasked.

VE: What might a person expect during their initiation for hope in terms of awareness or anything unusual?

IF: A very important thing to understand about all these initiations, as with all energy work, is that the effects will vary from one person to another. So the best attitude to have is one of openness without expectation. Having said that, probably the most common thing a person can expect to have is an increase in their awareness of the role that hope plays in their life, to have an increase in awareness of the ways in which they have not been hopeful, and to notice the ways in which they have allowed negative thought forms and negative emotion forms to influence their life. We are all influenced by these much more strongly than we realize. *Now it's important to understand that this and all the other star initiations are processes which require our conscious participation.* The Arcturian initiation will not magically turn you into a joyful, hopeful person. We need to learn to recognize and to resist the negative thoughts and emotions that we are habituated to. The energy won't do that for us; that's work we have to do. However, the energy will support us in our efforts.

VE: Now let me ask a general question that applies to all of the initiations. Do the spiritual masters that we already know, such as Buddha and Jesus, have anything to do with the masters in other star systems?

IF: Yes, very definitely. All of these exalted beings, both those we are familiar with on Earth and non-terrestrial, work for the same boss, so to speak, namely God. They are intimately aware of God's divine plan and work cooperatively to fulfill it.

VE: You said earlier that the Arcturians focus on and utilize what would be called a more feminine energy. Is there anything more you want to say about how that affects us today and where we're headed?

IF: The first thing to understand is that Christ energy is inherently balanced. It's both male and female. If you look at the historical Jesus, who is the foremost exemplar that we know of Christ Consciousness and Christ energy, you can see that in his life. The primary Arcturian gift for humanity, not so much at the present time but in the future, is the development of Christ Consciousness. What the Arcturians are doing now is building on the Sirian foundation and laying the framework for what will come to pass. Why? Because although Christ Consciousness is itself balanced, the manifestation that we see on our planet is unbalanced towards the masculine influence. As previously stated, the Arcturians can help us develop both the yin and yang aspects of Christ Consciousness, but are particularly adept at helping us develop the yin (feminine) aspect of Christ Consciousness.

VE: So it sounds like sometime during this next thousand years we are going to be evolving into the proper assimilation of more feminine energy to balance the predominant masculine.

IF: Correct. There's been more awareness in esoteric circles about the fact that the Seventh Ray is increasing its effect on our planet now. The Seventh Ray is associated with the divine feminine. Many of the changes that we've seen in individual consciousness and societal consciousness toward more balance, toward more accepting and honoring of the feminine, is because of the accentuated influence of the Seventh Ray. Although the ray doesn't originate with Arcturus, the Arcturians have a major responsibility in modulating its frequencies to fit different civilizations. Indeed, the masters from each of the star systems described in this book have such a responsibility for modulating one or more of the rays and they also always work in cooperation with masters from the other star systems.

VE: I find it interesting that the Arcturians, who bring the first of the seven energy blessings, should recognize the human need for hope, especially during our many current challenges. From the recent weather calamities, to economic difficulties, to warring factions within and between nations, many people feel overwhelmed and fearful. Thus, hope, the eternal antidote to confusion, chaos and adversity, comes as a heavenly gift to help us maintain our faith and positive attitude.

It is said that hope springs eternal. Let us be thankful this is so as we graciously accept the Arcturian energy blessing being offered at this time to help us to build a network of light and love around the world.

☆ ☆ ☆ ☆ ☆ ☆ ☆ ☆ ☆ ☆ ☆ ☆ ☆ ☆ ☆ ☆☆ ☆ ☆ ☆ ☆ ☆ ☆

Please remember to allow one week between this and the next initiation.

Chapter 6

POLARIS – THE BLESSING OF BREATH

Commentary by Irving

Before receiving this or any of the other star initiations, it is necessary to receive the *Subtle Body Fortification Attunement* and *Anti-Glamour Initiation* as explained on pages 69-74. Like the other star initiations, you can receive this initiation from Polaris by simply asking for it (after doing the *Subtle Body Fortification Attunement* and *Anti-Glamour Initiation*). It is recommended that you **read this chapter** before asking for and receiving this initiation. Like the other star initiations, it takes about an hour and a quarter to receive the entire initiation. Please refer to page 79 to review the star initiation process.

This Polarian initiation brings you the energy to work with your breathing. All spiritual traditions have recognized the spiritual significance of the breath. Indeed the English word "spirit" comes from a Latin word meaning "breath." The way in which we breathe affects our state of consciousness, both directly and indirectly, through influencing our subtle bodies.

This initiation has two interrelated purposes. First, it works over time to release holding patterns in the nervous system which prevent you from breathing in more varied ways. The sources of these holding patterns are our negative emotional and mental programming. Second, it enables your Higher Self to work more easily with your breathing to help you evolve personally and spiritually.

The initiation employs a gridwork system which it creates in an important energy center in the body interior near the top of the occipital bone (the bump slightly above the base of the skull). This center helps to control breathing and has been given many names in different cultures—for example, the Jade Pillow in Taoism, the Gate of the Four Winds in Huna, and the Moon Center in Hinduism. In all of these traditions it is correctly said that the yin energy of this center balances the overall yang energy of the brain. This balance corresponds to the way in which the yang energy of Polaris A is balanced by the yin energy of Polaris B (as we will see, Polaris is a double star.) There is a resonance between the energy center at the top of the occipital bone and the medulla oblongata, which governs important autonomic functions including respiration and circulation. When this center opens, your breathing varies naturally to fit the situation. It is important to realize that there is no one right way to breathe. We breathe differently when we are sitting, standing, running, playing tennis, swimming, meditating, etc.

This initiation enables your Higher Self to work with you more easily to affect your breathing for personal and spiritual evolution. This will happen automatically once you receive the initiation. However, you can benefit even more by consciously requesting your Higher Self to work with your breathing. Because the breath is the doorway to the Divine, one of the most useful things anyone (whether they have received this initiation or not) can do is to ask the Higher Self to work with the breath. After receiving this initiation you may notice changes in your breathing at any time; however, you are particularly likely to notice such changes when you are meditating. Be open to letting these changes be present, even if they seem unusual or even if they seem disturbing. *Remember that through the holding patterns in our breathing we repress emotions.* As these patterns are freed and the emotions start to come up, we may feel anxiety.

The previous Arcturian initiation for hope has as one of its effects increasing the amount of oxygen which your body can hold. This initiation continues that process by both increasing the amount of oxygen you can hold and increasing your ability to use it. Although each of the seven star initiations is useful in itself, they are designed primarily to work together to develop Christ Consciousness. This initiation facilitates the development of Christ Consciousness by facilitating a number of breathing patterns associated with that state. The most important common element in these patterns is the movement of the chest in such a way as to promote the free flow of energy through the heart chakra.

The masters who bring this initiation are associated with the star called Polaris, which is about 1600 times as bright as our Sun and is about 690 light-years distant from the Sun. It is the brightest star in the constellation Ursa Minor (the "Little Bear") and is the forty-ninth brightest star in the sky as seen from the Earth. The constellation Ursa Minor contains the group of stars commonly called the Little Dipper. The Little Dipper is actually not a constellation itself, but a distinctive group of stars called an "asterism."

It is not commonly realized that Polaris is actually a double star. If we look through a powerful enough telescope at what the naked eye sees as a single source of light, we see that there are actually two stars. The larger one is white and the smaller companion has a pale bluish tint.

To locate Polaris first find another well known asterism, namely the Big Dipper in the constellation Ursa Major. Then find the two stars at the end of the cup (these are known as the "pointer stars") and follow the line determined by these stars in a direction pointing away from the Big Dipper. The first bright star is Polaris.

Polaris is commonly known as the North Star (the name Polaris is short for Stella Polaris, which is Latin for Star of the North). This is the star that is nearest to the North Celestial Pole. If you can spot Polaris in the sky, you can always tell which way is north. In addition, the angle of Polaris above the horizon tells you your latitude on the Earth. For these reasons Polaris is the most important star for navigators and travelers.

Polaris is only temporarily the North Star. Because the

Earth is not perfectly spherical, the gravitational attraction of the Sun and the Moon cause the Earth's axis to undergo a motion called "precession." This motion is like the wobbling of a spinning top and results in a 14,000 year cycle in the identity of the pole star. In about 14,000 years Vega will be the North Star, and another 14,000 years after that, Polaris will again be the North Star.

In cultures throughout the world, Polaris is a symbol of constancy and faithfulness. Those who work with star energies have used the energies of Polaris to promote steadfastness on the emotional level and focus on the mental level. It supports the will, not in a forceful way, but through helping us to experience a combination of will and serenity through alignment with our Higher Self. It is particularly useful for group work since its energies can be used to maintain group unity and focus, but in a way which respects the individuality of group members.

Always remember that the energies of a star, even more than a person, contain many frequencies and so have many different uses. When you tune into the energy of a star you may well become aware of properties different then the ones commonly referred to in books. Thus the most commonly referred to properties of Polaris energies are probably the ones given above. However, this star is particularly multi-faceted and its energies can be used in many ways. The most important mission of the masters of Polaris is to facilitate the development of the Earth's brow chakra. The energies of Polaris combine particularly well with clear quartz and with water. A favorite focal point for the masters of Polaris is a large body of water such as the Amazon River.

Conversation between Virginia and Irving

VE: Let's start with a general understanding of the relationship between the masters on Polaris and planet Earth's evolution.

IF: One of the important things to realize about Polaris is that it is a very multifaceted energy that has been affecting

Earth's subtle body fields for eons. While it's true of star energies in general that they contain many frequencies, this is particularly true of Polaris, and so it has been used by different spiritual traditions in different ways. It plays a very major role in both Taoist and Huna traditions.

One of the main ways that Polaris has been used in the Taoist tradition is in working with the pineal gland, where the light from Polaris is directly absorbed into the pineal in order to accelerate spiritual evolution. Taoists also use Polarian energy to evoke the spiritual properties of the kidneys, including kindness. In Huna, Polaris is used to develop many properties of the throat chakra, particularly creativity. Still another use of Polarian energy is in cellular regeneration.

It's important to understand that when we talk about tuning into the energy of a star that we're not talking about just the physical light. When I previously used the term light, I was using it in a generic sense to refer to spiritual energy, not just physical energy. Be assured there's an act of consciousness which is involved, and this is one of the things that makes it difficult for people who are more scientifically oriented. They can't understand how the star could affect you with this much power because the energy, the physical light, that's coming from that star is so small. It's important to understand that what we're doing is not just working with the physical energy from Polaris, but through an act of consciousness we are tuning into the spiritual bodies of Polaris or whatever star we're contacting. A star, just like a human being, has successive layers of subtle bodies. It has a physical and etheric body, but it also has higher bodies as well, which are all important for us.

VE: Do you see any comparison between the Taoist and Huna energy applications in terms of regenerating our physical DNA strands? Would either of them really be affecting the physical experience? Most people today talk about going through this shift in their DNA.

IF: The effect of star energies, including Polaris, on the subtle energy fields of DNA is something that is primarily being understood in modern times. There are traditions which have worked with this, but they haven't done so with the integrated spiritual and scientific understanding that we have currently. In other words, ancient peoples did not know about DNA in the same way that we are now learning from modern science, and this illustrates the importance of integrating ancient teachings with both science and newer teachings that are coming into the planet.

We can't really ignore either the ancient or newer teachings. People with traditional spiritual perspectives often tend to look askance at what goes on in the New Age movement without understanding that there are legitimate new teachings coming through. On the other hand, there is reason why they look askance, and that is because many people in the New Age movement lack the serious grounding and the commitment to serious inner work that comes from working with classical traditions. They also frequently lack, to be blunt, very basic spiritual knowledge. For example, relating this to a Buddhist perspective, in the New Age movement, people would tend to be focused on the third and fourth parts of what the Buddha called the Four Noble Truths rather than the first and the second which talk about the reality of suffering in life and attachment as the cause of suffering. There's a tendency in the New Age movement to want to say that everything is "perfect" and ignore suffering. So as such, the Taoist and Huna traditions do not speak in terms of DNA.

VE: But a strength of the New Age movement is that it tends to more openly accept contemporary information.

IF: That's a testament to the progress that humanity has made. There's an unfortunate tendency for people to look on the negative side of where we are, but if you look at the broader picture humanity has made incredible progress, and in our own time we see a remarkable escalating interest in spirituality. Recently, during the same week, there was a cover article in Time magazine about angels and a major article inside Newsweek about angels. The interest that we see in angels is just one of the evidences of the growing interest that we see in spiritual development.

VE: You had mentioned that the masters on Polaris are able to work with the clear quartz and also water. I was wondering if our reception of the Polaris energies would be aided by either using quartz crystals while we're doing the hour and a quarter initiation session, or if being in the water physically would have any positive effect in receiving them during or after the initiation.

IF: Those things would have a slight effect; however, the initiations are so strong that easily 80 percent or more of the effect comes without the use of these external aids.

VE: You mentioned that they really like the Amazon River and I wondered whether large bodies of water like the Great Lakes, or even oceans, would also be suitable.

IF: Their liking of the Amazon River has more to do with the devic life which supports the Amazon than it has to do with the physical properties of the Amazon. Every major body of water has devas and nature spirits associated with it. The metaphysical properties of that water have to do not just with the physical properties of the water or the surrounding Earth and the atmosphere, but with the nature of the devic community which supports the ecosystem as well.

VE: Do the devas hold that energy for the physical planet?

IF: Yes, and looking at it from a purely energetic point of view, the frequencies that are in the devic community that support a particular ecosystem, whether it's a river or a mountain, relate to the culture in which that ecosystem occurs. In other words, there's a synergy between the energy of the devic community and the natural frequencies which are present in the spiritual energies of that culture.

VE: Are the Polarian energies more effective when they go to remote regions far away from large metropolitan areas?

IF: Yes, it's also true that the energies are less disrupted there than in our modern technological civilization.

VE: An interesting comment to me concerns how the energy of the Polarian initiation is going to help us breathe better during meditation—especially with the movement of the chest. Could you give us more information about the move-ment of the chest when we're receiving it, and what we might notice?

IF: When I was talking about an actual physical move-ment, I was referring to the fact that there's a connection between the state of Christ Consciousness and breathing. This is a kind of knowledge which has been mostly lost in modern times. It's certainly natural that there should be such a con-nection. We know that every spiritual tradition teaches techniques of breathing which are associated with the state of consciousness they consider to be "enlightenment." One thing that is distinctive about this initiation is that there is a gridwork system near the base of the skull, previously mentioned, through which you are more closely connected to your Higher Self. So your Higher Self can work with you in an ongoing way to facilitate your breathing in the interest of personal and spiritual growth.

There are many different ways that these breathing pat-terns might manifest depending upon a particular person, their individual nature, and their progress on their spiritual path. However, one common element in these different breathing patterns which promote Christ Consciousness is breathing so that the chest is relaxed, allowing a free flow of energy through the heart chakra. The opening of the heart chakra is absolutely crucial to the development of Christ Consciousness. So the breathing patterns which support the opening of the heart chakra are useful in themselves and also as a way to facilitate the development of Christ Consciousness.

VE: So are you saying a person wouldn't even have to know what shifts and changes were needed, the Higher Self would simply...

IF: That's correct. That's one of the beauties of this attunement. It's actually best to simply let the personality get out of the way and to avoid preconceptions about what these breathing patterns might be like. And one of the key things to understand is that *there is no one right way to breathe!* There are many different ways to breathe depending on the particular situation. Even if we're talking about the same situation, for example meditation, or even if we're talking about creating a specific state of consciousness, there are still different ways of breathing that are appropriate for different people to promote that state. The best thing that anyone can do is to get out of the way and let this attunement and your Higher Self work together to guide you. I'm not saying that consciously working with breathing is not helpful, studying breathing techniques can be extremely helpful, but there comes a time to just let go.

VE: So in other words you might follow a Hindu master, and he would tell you to breathe a certain way, or a Buddhist lama would put you in a certain situation, and you would be breathing their way. However, you're saying that while that technique may be useful, ultimately it might not be the best one?

IF: Yes, and it might not be what's right for the individual involved. People tend to choose breathing methods which perpetuate their patterns of holding emotion. Even people who are seriously interested in growth, and who need growth to feel whole, will choose methods which only open them up a little bit over breathing methods which will really open their holding patterns and thereby result in feelings of emotional threat.

This is one of the reasons why it's really necessary on the spiritual path to have a teacher, because we tend to adopt those beliefs and practices which perpetuate our blocks and our holding patterns. Depending on the particular person, breathing methods other than those they have studied may actually be more helpful or may simply be a valuable complement to those they've used already. I find that people tend to become very opinionated about breathing. They tend to think that there's a certain method and only that is the one right way. The truth is, as I've said, that there is no one right way to breathe. That truth is particularly emphasized by the Polarians, who are masters of the breathing process.

VE: Let me ask you this. What physical or nonphysical

forms do the Polarian folks have that breath would have been so important that they became masters of that process?

IF: I don't really think it has so much to do with their physical form as with the spiritual properties of breath. I haven't really talked to the masters from Polaris in depth about why the breath was so important, but one thing which I do know is that there's considerable emphasis on group consciousness in the Polaris spiritual tradition. Earlier, one of the things that I mentioned was that Polaris is a particularly useful energy for working with groups of people because it can help maintain group focus while simultaneously respecting the individuality of persons in the group. In the tradition of Huna, into which I've been initiated, there's a saying that we all breathe the same air but each of us must take our breath individually. The breath is a wonderful metaphor for both our separateness and our inter-relatedness.

VE: Then the Polarians are using breath as a tool to help raise consciousness. Now I have a question about the energy center near the base of the skull, and how it relates to the medulla oblongata.

IF: Yes, the Jade Pillow is a subtle energy center and it is interrelated to the medulla oblongata, but it should not be identified with the medulla oblongata. In effect there is a very basic point here which is that the energy centers in the subtle bodies are just that, they're in the subtle bodies and not in the physical body. A common misconception is that the chakras are in the physical body rather than the subtle bodies. People frequently tend to identify a chakra with the associated nerve plexus. But the nerve plexus is not the chakra. No one in the history of medical dissection ever found a thousand-petal lotus structure in the top of the human head.

The crown chakra does not exist in the physical body; it is in the subtle bodies. Each chakra is associated not just with a nerve plexus but also with a gland and an organ. It's just as much a mistake to identify the chakra with the nerve plexus as it would be to identify the chakra with the organ or the gland.

VE: Let me come back to what you said in the introduction. You said— whether it's the Jade Pillow or the Gate of the Four Winds or the Moon Center—that the yin energy of this center balances the overall yang energy of the brain. So why is the brain's energy yang?

IF: If you look at the energy of the brain as a whole it is noticeably more assertive than receptive because the primary function of the brain from a biological perspective is to control and manipulate our environment and that prejudices it in the assertive direction.

VE: So how does this center near the base of the skull balance the energy of the brain?

IF: From a subtle energy perspective, that center helps to distribute the yin energy of the primary yin channel in the subtle body, a vertical channel located to the left of the spine called ida in Hinduism.

VE: Is this center connected with what we call the soul input, the intuition?

IF: That center near the base of the skull is definitely connected with intuition and with the unconscious mind. It's also very much connected with the Moon which is why it has been called the Moon Center. There are traditions such as Huna, for example, where practitioners go out on a moonlit night and absorb energy from the Moon into that center to affect their dreams. So it's very much a center that is connected with our unconscious and with our intuition.

VE: How does the subtle energy from the Jade Pillow center, near the base of the physical body's skull, connect with the rest of the body?

IF: It does so by traveling through the energy channels in the subtle bodies which interconnect the innumerable centers. If we look at the physical body we see that there are what we might call centers, such as glands and organs—and that these are also channels which interconnect centers. Examples of channels in the physical body are nerves and blood vessels. Similarly, in the subtle bodies we have energy centers and energy channels. In the Hindu tradition the channels are referred to as nadis. The word nadi comes from a Hindu root meaning "to flow." It is through these channels that subtle energy flows. So energy from the Jade Pillow flows through the nadis in all directions but not equally. For example, there is a particularly strong flow of energy from this subtle body center to the physical body's medulla oblongata—a part of the brain that helps regulate breathing, the circulatory system, etc.

VE: Since we're so intellectually oriented in Western society, have we interfered with the natural balance of yin and yang energies in our subtle bodies?

IF: It certainly is possible to interfere with the natural processes of subtle energy transfer just as it's possible through unwise decisions about the amount of exercise, sleep, or one's diet, to interfere with the flow of energy in the physical body. It is true that as a culture we are very unbalanced and have too much yang energy.

VE: So if we meditated more would this produce more yin energy and help us balance out?

IF: Yes, this is one of the many benefits of meditation—it will help to regularize the flow of subtle energy. Meditation is really the key to everything. It's both the primary key to spiritual growth and also a master key in affecting energy flow throughout the body.

VE: So, Irving, when you see people clairvoyantly, can you tell if their Jade Pillow center is working properly? How would a person know if it was operating effectively?

IF: Yes, I can see it, and I can tell how the center is functioning for that person. It's very difficult for someone who isn't energy sensitive to judge these things for themselves. That's why the use of a shakti for balancing one's centers is critical.

VE: In addition to individual differences, do you notice differences between cultures with respect to the functioning of the Jade Pillow or other energy centers?

IF: There are definitely cultural differences with respect to the activity of certain centers. To give one example, there are two centers located in the head associated with mental functioning which have been commonly called the brow chakra. One of these centers is located between the eyebrows. The other center is located at the level of the middle of the forehead. In Hinduism, the center between the eyebrows has been called the Ajna center. And the center that is located in the middle of the forehead has been called the Soma center. Now the truth is that there are chakras in both locations; that's why there's this great difference of opinion as to where the brow chakra is actually located. When I say they are chakras what I mean is that they both have petal structures. A chakra is not simply an energy center. *Some people use the term chakra just to mean energy center, but what characterizes a chakra is that it has a petal structure.*

It's very interesting that most people will have one of these centers much more active than the òther. It's rare to find someone who has them both very active, although that is actually the direction that our development leads us. In India most people have the center between the eyebrow more active, whereas in the United States most people have the center that is in the middle of the forehead more active. Just as different individuals have different paths, the same thing is true of cultures. Different systems of energy work are appropriate for different cultures. Of course this is a generalization because we are all individuals.

VE: Returning to the Jade Pillow center, does the fact that it is associated with respiration mean that someone who has trouble breathing—such as asthma or emphysema—is having problems with this center?

IF: There are many different reasons why people have different breathing patterns and different problems in breathing. The openness and functioning of that center is a major factor in such differences, but it's certainly not the only factor. For example, a person who has been exposed to asbestos will likely suffer from breathing problems, but this is a purely physical breathing problem, and is not caused by factors in their subtle anatomy.

VE: Since I understand that planet Earth also "breathes," are the Polarians affecting this process in any way?

IF: There is a rhythmic contraction and expansion of the Earth's subtle energy fields that distributes energy throughout her gridwork system, analogous to the contraction and expansion of the human lungs. The Polarians are facilitating the evolution of this planetary "breathing," particularly as it relates to the development of group consciousness. The Earth has the equivalent of a Jade Pillow center, and much of the Polarians' work is accomplished through helping this center. Although we've talked about subtle energy, we must remember that no amount of subtle energy can make up for air which has been degraded by environmental toxins. All human and animal life is jeopardized when we don't take responsibility for the quality of our unique planet's oxygen.

VE: Yes, breath is the most fundamental aspect, not only of our personal life but as you say, of all human and animal life! So I agree our responsibility as citizens not only requires concern about the air quality of our individual countries but of the entire Earth. We must never forget that we are global citizens and that toxic air in one area can affect vast numbers of people. Recent history has already shown us the devastating results of Chernobyl, the burning oils fields of the Gulf War, and the extensive fires in the East Indies which demonstrate that we are bound together as planetary citizens. What we must now do is to get all agencies within governments and between governments to conserve the vital trees which exchange our exhaled carbon dioxide with pure oxygen from the plant kingdom.

We have been told we have dominion here on Earth— that we are stewards responsible for maintaining Earth's pristine nature. As long as we have human breath, let us dedicate that gift of physical life to our stewardship responsibilities, not only to one another, but to our beautiful homeland and its myriad life forms.

☆ ☆ ☆ ☆ ☆ ☆ ☆ ☆ ☆ ☆ ☆ ☆ ☆ ☆ ☆ ☆☆ ☆ ☆ ☆ ☆ ☆ ☆

Please remember to allow one week between this and the next initiation.

Chapter 7

PLEIADES – THE BLESSING OF LOVE

Commentary by Irving

Before receiving this or any of the other star initiations, it is necessary to receive the *Subtle Body Fortification Attunement* and *Anti-Glamour Initiation* as explained on pages 69-74. Like the other star initiations, you can receive this Pleiadian initiation by simply asking for it (after doing the *Subtle Body Fortification Attunement* and *Anti-Glamour Initiation*). It is recommended that you **read this chapter** before asking for and receiving this initiation. Like the other star initiations, it takes about an hour and a quarter to receive the entire initiation. Please refer to page 79 to review the star initiation process.

The purpose of the Pleiadian initiation is to assist in opening your heart chakra in a safe, integrated, and organic way. In general the most effective and safest way to open a chakra is to do it, as this initiation does, through the divinely guided intelligence of shakti. Many popular exercises for the chakras force and keep the petals open prematurely; these almost always interfere with the functioning of the chakra and often injure it, sometimes permanently. As the heart chakra becomes more open, all of its natural functions become more developed.

One important function of the heart chakra is to balance and harmonize the other chakras. Its position in the center of the chakra system reflects this function. From a spiritual perspective the most important function of the heart chakra is to help us experience greater love and compassion for ourselves and others. Ultimately the love it helps us to experience is the unconditional love of Christ Consciousness. Like the other star initiations, this initiation is included because it has multiple levels of more immediate benefits in addition to helping with the more long-term goal of developing Christ Consciousness. Some likely benefits include greater love and compassion for yourself and others, increased serenity, and profound connection to nature (a major Pleiadian value).

When we talk about the heart chakra opening, we are referring quite literally to the collective degree of openness of its 12 petals. It is important to distinguish between four things which are often confused with one another in the popular literature about chakras. These are:

1) the degree of openness of a chakra
2) the amount of energy in a chakra
3) the amount of energy in a chakra *relative* to another chakra or chakras
4) the actual *functioning* of a chakra

As an analogy, consider the amount of sunlight in several flowers on the same bush. With respect to a particular flower we might consider how open the petals are, how much sunlight is in that flower, how much sunlight is in that flower compared to other flowers on the bush, and the actual functioning of the flower. Later in this chapter additional explanations about these distinctions and the way they're important will be given.

The Pleiades (pronounced 'plee-uh-deez) is a cluster of stars in the constellation Taurus, about 400 light-years from our solar system. It consists of several hundred bright, hot stars that were all formed at the same time within a large cloud of interstellar dust and gas. The Pleiades is accompanied by a blue haze that is caused by a very fine dust which still remains and reflects a blue light from the stars.

Classically seven of the Pleiades are said to be observable with the naked eye, though different observers have reported different numbers of stars, depending on visual acuity and viewing conditions. In Greek mythology the stars of the Pleiades are associated with the seven daughters of the titan Atlas and the oceanid Pleione: Alcyone, Maia, Electra, Merope, Taygete, Celaeno, and Sterope. The brightest star of the Pleiades, Alcyone, is nearly 1000 times brighter than our Earth's Sun, while the faintest is less than 1/100th as bright.

The Pleiades is one of the brightest star clusters visible in the northern hemisphere and it is certainly the most famous. In modern time the Pleiades has probably been the subject of more astronomical photographs then any other object in the heavens outside of our solar system. In ancient times the Pleiades was known and revered in many cultures. The heliacal (near dawn) rising of the Pleiades in spring of the Northern hemisphere often signaled the opening of seafaring and farming seasons, just as the morning setting of the Pleiades in autumn signaled the season's end. These rising and setting times were often the occasion of religious festivals. It was commonly believed in ancient times that many significant events had happened either at the rising or the setting of the Pleiades. Tradition has it that the Buddha was born during the rising of the Pleiades and that Atlantis sank during its setting.

Like the Arcturians, the Pleiadeans work with Christ Consciousness as a whole, but focus more on the feminine, yin aspects. Sirius and Arcturus and the Pleiades form an important energetic triangle for the development of Christ Consciousness. Yin frequencies from both Arcturus and the Pleiades (particularly Alcyone) act to balance the very yang frequencies of Sirius. The yin frequencies from the Pleiades work primarily with the odd numbered rays while the yin frequencies from Arcturus work primarily with the even numbered rays. The fact that it takes two sources to balance the yang frequencies of Sirius is a testament to the power of Sirius. We will discuss the great importance of Sirius with respect to Christ Consciousness in the chapter dealing with the Sirian star initiation.

Because the full development of Christ Consciousness involves working with multiple interrelated levels of reality, many different spiritual guides are needed to help humanity in its development. Here are four major areas in which the Pleiadeans are particularly adept:

1) With the development of Christ Consciousness there comes a dramatic shift in the functioning of the heart chakra. This includes a quantitative shift in the previously present ability to harmonize, balance and direct the other chakras. It also includes the unfolding of latent potentials within the heart chakra to play a major role in directing the development of Christ Consciousness in a general way.

2) The Pleiadeans are adept at using one of the characteristic capacities of the Cosmic Christ in what has been called "universal projection"—the ability to project the Cosmic Christ's heart chakra energy equally to every point in the universe. The Pleiadeans are proficient at helping advanced students of Christ Consciousness access this universal presence of the Cosmic Christ. When this is accomplished, there is an extraordinary feeling that every single point is sacred and equally the center of the universe.

3) In order for the energies of Christ Consciousness to be fully effective they must be anchored at the cellular level. The Pleiadeans play an important ongoing role in working at the cellular and sub-cellular levels, including pivotal work with the DNA strands.

4) Esoteric traditions throughout the world have recognized that hidden within physical light are remarkable secrets about the structure of the universe, as well as a metaphorical ladder which can be used to access progressively higher states of consciousness. One way (but not the only way) to view light is as a field of Christ Consciousness. In the future the Pleiadeans will help humanity to use certain key frequencies in physical light to build what has been called the "Christ Body" which is latent within everyone's subtle energy field. There is an interplay between the development of the Christ Body and the development of Christ Consciousness—each promotes the other. The ancient Maya worked extensively with this. In the future the Pleiadeans will also help humanity to use other frequencies of physical light to activate sites on the

subtle bodies of the DNA strands. One of the important functions of these sites (energy centers whose disc shape resembles that of a satellite TV dish) is to help us to better receive and integrate energies from different non-terrestrial civilizations that are meant to guide the spiritual development of humanity.

Conversation between Virginia and Irving

VE: The Pleiades is certainly attracting the attention of the New Age community, and from what you've said, there's a good reason. Will you summarize why the Pleiades is so significant for humanity and why it is particularly relevant at this time?

IF: The single most important point about the Pleiades energy is that it is one of the three star systems destined to most help humanity in the development of Christ Consciousness, the others being Sirius and Arcturus. In the future, the Arcturians will be the more significant yin carrier of Christ Consciousness to humanity, whereas at the present time the Pleiadians are the more important in this respect. The Pleiades is particularly relevant at this time because it is involved in two of the most significant trends presently affecting us— the increasing role of the divine feminine in bringing about balance on our planet and the fact that humanity is getting increasingly close to a quantum jump in our manifestation of Christ Consciousness.

Through Christ Consciousness we can recognize that each point in the universe is a manifestation of God and that each point is equally divine. This means that we are here to celebrate the holiness of the Earth just as much as we are here to celebrate the immaterial aspects of God.

Pleiadian spirituality has a very deep understanding of the sanctity of nature, which is a basic aspect of Christ Consciousness. The Pleiadeans can be of much help to us at this time when the environment is so threatened. We can see, through his use of many agricultural metaphors, that the historical Jesus had a deep love of nature and a keen appreciation of the relationship between the Earth and our spirituality. Many people have sensed an increased luminosity in nature which comes from the infusion of nature with Christ Consciousness. This luminosity is due in part to the influx of energies which the Pleiadeans are sending to the Earth's gridwork.

VE: Since you spoke about the Pleiadeans in connection with nature, are there any present Earth cultures expressing their influence?

IF: The Pleiades plays a major role in Hawaiian thought through the Huna tradition, and there are certain guides which the Hawaiians believe come from the Pleiades—for example, the Menehune. Although they are often said to be small-statured people, the Menehune are actually devas, that is, nature spirits.

VE: Is it your understanding that the precursor of Huna and the Hawaiian tradition was Lemuria, and that was also a focus of the Pleiadeans?

IF: Oh, very definitely. The Hawaiians have many stories about what they call the motherland or Lemuria, and Hawaiian energies bear a very striking similarity to Lemurian energies. So yes, Lemurians were also very definitely influenced by the Pleiadeans.

VE: Are there any other geographical or cultural regions to mention? I'm thinking of something I read that indicated the Philippines had a very high relationship with the healing aspect during the time of Lemuria, and of course today we see people going to the Philippines to be healed by psychic surgeons, etc. Would it have been likely that the attitude of healing is also important in present day Pleiadian thinking, or is that just the way it played out down here?

IF: Yes, the Pleiadeans are very talented at healing, and helping other cultures understand the principles of healing through nature is an important focus of their teachings. I believe there is a connection with the Philippines. Another culture which was very much influenced by the Pleiadeans was the ancient Mayan culture. They also had some very remarkable understandings about healing.

VE: Can you explain more about why the Pleiadeans are using what we call the yin or feminine frequencies?

IF: In the development of Christ Consciousness, both yin and yang energies are important. The fact that the Pleiadeans are emphasizing the yin frequencies doesn't mean that those are more important. However, it's necessary to balance the fact that in our Western cultures we have too much yang energy.

VE: Shifting to the topic of chakras, which you introduced earlier on, could you give us more background information about the chakras?

IF: Before getting into the details, I want to emphasize that the underlying attitude with which one approaches understanding and developing the chakras can have far reaching effects, for good or for harm. The key to having the most beneficial attitude is appreciating that the development of a chakra is an organic, evolutionary process. It is all too easy to think of "opening a chakra" as a mechanical process, much like opening the lid of a jar. It is important to realize that a chakra is part of a living being—namely you! Just as the physical matter which makes up your kidneys is living matter as opposed to inanimate matter, so the subtle matter which makes up chakras is living subtle matter rather than inanimate subtle matter. You should treat your chakras with the same care and respect that you would treat any part of your physical body. The safest and most effective way to work with your chakras is to use a shakti.

As mentioned earlier, a chakra resembles a flower, both in its structure and in its functioning. Since I just referred to the structure of a chakra, the first thing I should emphasize is that chakras are made up of subtle matter. The use of the term "energy center" in referring to chakras has misled many people into thinking that chakras are somehow made up of pure energy. A chakra *conducts* energy, but the chakra itself is made up of subtle matter. The subtle matter of a chakra resembles a flower with parts, traditionally labeled "petals" in Eastern cultures, because they look like the petals of a flower. **(See Illustration #4)** Like a flower's petals, they are arranged in layers. Since a chakra is spinning rather than stationary, a good way to visualize a chakra is as a spinning flower. This spinning or rotation elongates the subtle matter of the chakra to give it an overall conical or funnel appearance.

A chakra also resembles a flower in the way that it develops. As we evolve spiritually, the petals of the chakra open up in the way that the petals of a flower open up. There is a positive feedback loop between the growth of our consciousness and the opening of our chakras. For example, as we become

Illustration #4 - Your heart chakra has four layers of petals, each layer consisting of three petals. At the center of the petals is a projection of your monad, which is the carrier of your divine individuality.

more loving, the petals of our heart chakra become more open and this openness in turn makes it easier for us to become more loving. There are also various kinds of exercises and energy work which can be done to encourage a chakra to open, provided they are done properly. It is primarily the misunderstanding of these exercises that has led to confusion. If not understood, these exercises can create problems, even serious problems, for those doing them.

VE: Given that the safest and most effective way to develop your chakras is through the use of shakti, could you give us an example of an exercise that can cause problems if not done properly.

IF: A common exercise for the heart chakra is to visualize it coming open. The main usefulness of this exercise is to *encourage* the heart chakra to open. It does not actually cause much opening of the petals during the period when the exercise is being done because this opening is an evolutionary process. Another effect of doing this exercise is that the energy of the will and the energy of the thought used in the exercise energize or stimulate the heart chakra. The increased energy which this exercise brings to the heart chakra has only a slight effect on opening it; the main effect on opening it comes over time from the "creative visualization" aspect of the exercise. One of the four confusions to which I referred earlier is mistaking energizing a chakra for opening a chakra: the two are not the same. In the short run the main effect of this opening visualization exercise is to energize the heart chakra; but many people like this feeling and do the exercise for too long a time period. This overstimulates the heart chakra and can lead to a variety of problems, including heart disease. *Let me emphasize that there is nothing intrinsically wrong with this exercise; the problem comes from doing it too long.* Just as physical exercise can by beneficial when done for the right amount of time but can overstrain a muscle if done for too long, so can subtle energy exercise be beneficial if done for the right amount of time but be harmful if done for too long.

Energizing or stimulating a chakra gives us more life

energy and the result can feel pleasant. This energizing is fine as long as we don't *over* stimulate the chakra; however, most people can't tell where the danger zone begins.

It's important to understand that stimulation accentuates our pre-existing patterns rather than helping us to develop new patterns. The purpose of opening a chakra is to help us to develop new patterns; and in the case of opening the heart chakra this helps us to become more loving. The process of opening a chakra to change our consciousness is an organic one that can't be hurried! I've often said that you can't make a flower grow more rapidly by prying its petals open. It's also important to understand that the primary way we get our heart chakra to open is by actually practicing becoming a more loving person, *and no amount of visualization or energy work can substitute for this.* If you're going to use energy work to help your chakras open, the best way is to use a shakti because it "knows" exactly how much to work on each chakra and in what way. Using a shakti will help you to avoid the harm which misapplication of many commonly used practices can lead to.

VE: Now that you've explained the difference between opening a chakra and energizing a chakra, can you comment on the amount of energy a chakra should have? What is the proper balance and ratio that's needed in the system from one chakra to the other?

IF: First let me say that you can't presume that there's too much energy in a chakra just by looking at that one chakra alone. I've seen cases of an energy worker putting his/her hands over just a person's solar plexus chakra, for example, and reporting that the person had an overcharged solar plexus. What the energy worker is failing to take into account is that the person may have a very strong energy field in general and that all of that person's chakras have a great deal of charge in them. The amount of charge that the solar plexus chakra should have will vary from one person to another—and similarly for all the other chakras. But it *is* important that the amount of charge in each of the chakras be nearly equal.

Many systems of spiritual development denigrate the

lower chakras and the practices of these systems result in the upper chakras being overcharged. The lower chakras are there for a reason, however, and when they're spiritualized they function in a way which is in harmony with the spiritualization of the upper channels. Having too much charge in the upper chakras relative to the lower chakras can cause health problems, as in the earlier example I gave of how an overcharged heart chakra can lead to heart problems. In fact it's not uncommon for gurus in traditions that are very heart chakra oriented to die from heart problems because they have overcharged their heart chakras relative to the other chakras.

Many times people create energy imbalances by meditating on or doing exercises with a particular chakra or chakras out of proportion to the others. (I emphasize again that the best way to work with your chakras is to use a shakti because then you avoid all these kinds of problems.) If you're going to meditate on or do the more common kinds of energy exercises with your chakras, I strongly recommend working with all your chakras equally. Everyone has some kind of imbalance in their chakra system, and people who don't work on their chakras equally have a tendency to work on those chakras that will perpetuate their imbalances. For example, people who overemphasize the quality of will relative to love typically have overdeveloped solar plexus chakras. Carrying a lot of charge in their solar plexus helps them to feel secure and so if they choose to work with just one chakra, more often than not it is their solar plexus chakra. However, working on their solar plexus chakra out of proportion to the others just perpetuates their imbalance.

VE: Is there anything else you would like to share regarding the functioning of a chakra?

IF: Chakras are very complex and their functioning can be compared to a symphony orchestra. Each of the instruments may be perfectly tuned and yet they might not function harmoniously. In a similar way, each of the chakras can be open and can have the appropriate amount of charge, yet they still might not function in an integrated manner. When people work with the chakras they generally tend to focus on just one at a time, even though the chakras function together. Furthermore, they function in groups of three, four, etc. D.K. tells us that if you want to understand how the chakras function it's particularly important to look at *triangles* of chakras, or groups of three. Yet most chakra books don't even begin to talk about this.

VE: Considering that the Pleidian initiation is the blessing of love, and relative to the heart, can you give an example of a triangle involving the heart chakra?

IF: There are many triangles that we can form with the heart chakra because it links together so many levels of reality. For example, when the heart chakra, the throat chakra and the brow chakra triangulate this facilitates intuitive understanding.

VE: So let's say all the chakras are functioning the way they should, both individually and in groups. What happens then?

IF: Then the chakra system can fulfill its ultimate purpose, which is to help us ascend to higher states of consciousness—and to God.

VE: Regarding ascension, there are some beings called the Hathors now channeling through Tom Kenyon, who say in the book <u>The Hathor Material: Messages from an Ascended Civilization</u>, that a million of them were able to ascend into a higher frequency, taking their physical bodies with them by using love and sound frequencies. Do you think it's possible that in the generations ahead, people will literally ascend in the sense of being able to take their physical bodies with them into the frequencies that lie beyond the third dimension?

IF: I think eventually that happens for a person on an individual basis, but that the wonderful example of the Hathors is not the most common scenario. And I also think that for most people it happens at a much further point in their spiritual evolution than is often thought.

VE: It's important to realize that physical ascension is different than the consciousness aspect which is already in a constant state of growth and expansion—right?

IF: Yes. One of the remarkable things about our consciousness is that it can expand so much, as well as travel so easily to other times, to other spaces, to other dimensions.

VE: Regarding the subject of ascension, my concern is that many people want to substitute physical ascension for ascension of consciousness. They want to take their body and leave physical life. Other people want somebody to come and save them—perhaps put them in a starship and take them far away from here. My own guidance has always been that we're here to integrate spiritual consciousness with physical matter. Therefore, leaving the physical planet would remove us from our responsibility.

IF: I very much agree! I think that we're meant to become enlightened in a body, not outside of a body—in daily life, not outside of daily life. There's a tendency in Western culture to denigrate matter, and I think that the people who believe that they must ascend in order to become realized are falling victim to that belief. Spiritual evolution is not about transcending matter, but about integrating matter with spirit. Meister Eckhardt said, "The soul loves the body." Saint Augustine indicated that the soul and the body are so complementary that God could not have created the soul without also creating the body.

Many people want to ascend. They believe that by leaving their body they will automatically accelerate their spiritual evolution or will intrinsically experience happiness. If a person is unable to accept the full divinity and joy of the present moment in a physical body, they will carry that inability with them into a body of light. Because light exists at different frequencies, a person could be just as dissatisfied with a low frequency light-body as with a physical body. What really must change is the attitude of dissatisfaction.

VE: That's not to say we can't use consciousness to improve our physical conditions and the conditions of our planetary life.

IF: Of course not. It's simply to say that the solution is a change in consciousness, not a change in form. I believe that people do ascend, but *any change of form is the ultimate result of the change in consciousness.* Ironically, a sure sign that one's consciousness has not shifted is having a dire need to ascend.

There's an old Jewish story about a man who's lived his whole life in one town, and he's thinking of moving to a village just five miles down the road. He goes to the rabbi and says, "Rabbi, I'm thinking of moving after all these years. Tell me what the people in the next village are like." The rabbi says, "Well, tell me son, what are the people in this village like?" He answers, "Oh, they're very mean; they're very thoughtless. Why do you think I'm moving?" And the rabbi replies, "Well, you'll find the people in the next town are just the same." Later in the day another lifelong villager asks that same question, and the rabbi says, "Well, son, tell me what the people in this village are like." He replies, "Oh, they're wonderful; they're the most beautiful, loving people that I've ever known. That's why it's so hard for me to move." The rabbi replies, "Well, my son, you'll find the people in the next village are just the same." If you are dissatisfied with life in this dimension or in a physical body, and you move into another dimension or move into a body of light, you're going to be equally dissatisfied. The solution is not changing where you live or even changing your physical form; it's changing your consciousness!

VE: How is it we can live in a world where disasters are occurring and wars are going on and still maintain a positive attitude? There needs to be something constructive in life so we don't lose the sense of the greater purposes for which we've come.

IF: One of my favorite poets is Walt Whitman, who has a wonderful line in one of his poems that says we have to learn to be both in and out of the game. And that's really the answer. As human beings we are partly in the realm of time and partly in the eternal realm. We must be enough in the realm of time to be involved with our fellow human beings and to care what is happening; otherwise, we've lost our humanity. But we must also be in the realm of the eternal enough so that we can have a divine patience about this process unfolding in the way that it should. There's a wonderful comment in the Baghavad Gita where Krishna says to Arjuna that he has no need to take action and yet he acts ceaselessly.

VE: Right. Now I'd like to ask you about something you said earlier regarding frequencies of physical light that can be used to activate sites on the DNA subtle body strands.

IF: *It was intended from the beginning that humanity not evolve just by itself but in cooperation with spiritual beings on other planets.* This is true not just of humanity but of people on those other planets who are in turn helped by elder civilizations, civilizations that were more evolved spiritually. On the *subtle* body of a DNA strand (not on the physical DNA) there are 12 ray sites and these sites become active at a certain point in human evolution. Each enables a person to tune in more clearly to energies that are coming from one of the civilizations from which we are meant to receive guidance. I believe that for humanity as a whole, these ray sites may not become active for many centuries.

VE: So you're suggesting we need to grasp the difference between subtle body DNA influence and our physical DNA?

IF: Actually I believe that the current information about there being 12 strands of DNA was perhaps meant to be this information. In other words, the people who received information that there were 12 DNA strands assumed that it meant 12 physical strands. From a metaphysical point of view it doesn't really make sense to me to talk about 12 *physical* strands of DNA because the basic principle by which the phenomenal world is organized is the principle of duality: night and day, hot and cold, etc. In our bodies we see that if we have more than one of something we have two. For instance we have two kidneys—the kidney on the right side is more yang and the one on the left side which is more yin. Now all of this duality is reflective of the fact that the primordial ray of creation, the Kav ray as it is called in Kabbalah, has a yin aspect and a yang aspect. Since everything comes from this primordial ray, everything in the universe has a yin aspect and a yang aspect. If you put your consciousness into the DNA strands, one of them is yin and one of them is yang, and there is a very clear connection to the primordial yin and yang in the Kav ray. As we evolve spiritually, centers of energy— whether chakras, glands or DNA—rise in vibrational rate, but do not multiply numerically.

VE: Assuming you're correct, are some of the 12 subtle body ray sites beginning to activate now? If so, would that affect our chakras and our physical life experience?

IF: My understanding of the way the process is meant to work is that in the future when the sites are activated, a person becomes much more receptive to non-terrestrial energies, each site being associated with one set of energies. So the activation of the site does not directly affect the chakra system. However, the energies that will be absorbed as a result of that activation will definitely have a very strong effect.

VE: Then let's look more closely at the 12 DNA *subtle* energy sites. What do you know about them?

IF: Some of these 12 DNA subtle sites will be activated by non-terrestrial civilizations that you would naturally expect and recognize, such as the Sirians and the Pleiadeans. But some of them involve civilizations that we are meant to contact very far into the future, and it has actually not yet been revealed to humanity what some of these civilizations are. Although it would certainly be interesting to speculate who they are, at this point it would definitely be just speculation.

VE: So in other words, we're not promising that if you invite these particular seven energy blessings from the stars, offered in this book, that they will necessarily open those DNA sites?

IF: No, no. As I was saying earlier this will happen for humanity as a whole very much in the future. It's at least centuries away.

VE: Still, by absorbing as much as we can of whatever is offered to us now, this continues the support of where we're eventually going to be and when we're supposed to be there?

IF: Absolutely. Anyone who participates in the seven initiations that are outlined in this book is a pioneer in this process. By carrying these energies, they are helping the evolution of humanity. Just by being in a room with other people and having other people be exposed to these energies they are helping the evolution of humanity. There's also another principle at work here which is that the energies which the Spiritual Hierarchy can send to our planet are dependent upon the receptivity and the resonance of the energies already here. In other words, they must operate under their own rules. Every organization, even the Spiritual Hierarchy, has rules which it has to operate under if it is to survive. The way their rules work it's much easier for them to be permitted to send an energy to this planet if some precursor or some form of it already exists than if it's totally new.

VE: Are you saying that the Earth's gridwork has to be at a certain frequency before we could possibly handle these initiations?

IF: For these particular energies, no. However, it is true that in some cases for certain energies to come into the planet there is a precondition that the gridwork be evolved to a certain level.

VE: Do you know if that grid is shifting energetically at the present time?

IF: The subtle energy gridwork of the Earth is shifting very dramatically. It's a truism in the New Age that everything is speeding up and that more and more energies are coming into the planet. In this case it's very true. There's a positive feedback loop between our evolution and the fact that higher and higher vibrational energies are coming in. These incoming energies help us to evolve, and the fact that we're evolved to a certain point means that we can accept higher energies which in turn help us to evolve even further. So it's in the nature of this process that at a certain point things start going faster and faster. It's an exponential curve. At a certain point the curve really starts to take off. So that's what we're experiencing. That evolution speeds up exponentially is true in every cycle of creation .

VE: I was thinking about the zero point information mentioned by Gregg Braden and about the fact that Mother Earth herself is breathing or pulsating at a faster and faster rate. Is that because of the grids or is that because of a different energy that we don't know about yet?

IF: When we talk about the gridwork of the Earth, that term can be used in two ways. It can refer to the electromagnetic energy lines or it can refer to the subtle bodies of the Earth. There's a connection between the subtle body gridwork system of the Earth and the electromagnetic gridwork system of the physical Earth. There are many points to consider about this. One of them is that we need to prevent distortions from technology affecting the electromagnetic field of the Earth because that can produce distortions in the subtle body gridwork, and even more importantly in our own subtle bodies. The second point is that although there is an interrelationship between the electromagnetic gridwork and the subtle body gridwork, it's actually more important to understand how they are independent of each other. It is vital to know that the *subtle* body gridwork can evolve much faster than we can produce changes in the electromagnetic gridwork

It's analogous to the situation with a human being. As a human being evolves spiritually there certainly are changes in the physical body; however, the most dramatic changes take place in the subtle bodies. The subtle bodies are much more malleable and pliable than the physical body. A few hours of high level energy work can change the subtle bodies more than years of exercise or even plastic surgery can change the physical body. So it's very important to understand that when we're talking about spiritual evolution we're talking about changes in the subtle bodies more than we're talking about changes in the physical body. It is again true that changes in the physical body take place, but there's a tendency in our culture to confuse the physical level of reality with the spiritual level of reality. I see one example of that in what we were talking about previously, namely the 12 strands of DNA. In my opinion, it's not necessary to have 12 physical DNA strands anymore than it is necessary to have more than two kidneys or two lungs to evolve spiritually.

VE: So many people today are becoming ill and suffering from some unhealthy condition. I'd like your comments on what effect these star initiatory energies may have on our physical health. Can humanity expect any improvement in physical health because of them?

IF: Naturally the primary emphasis of these initiations is spiritual. Of course the spiritual is not divorced from our state of mind and our emotions, which we know can have a very profound effect on the body. We were talking earlier about the connection between emotional isolation and heart disease. Although these initiations are not intended to directly impact the physical health, it's certainly possible that they could do so. For example, people who experience greater love for themselves and for other people may well experience some shift in their health. However, it's important to understand that *the spiritual life is its own reward.* There is no guarantee that by embarking on a spiritual life that life on the physical plane is going to improve. There's no guarantee that you're going to be healthy or that you're going to become rich or famous, and this is totally appropriate. If there were some sort of guaranteed connection between pursuing spiritual development and welfare on the physical plane then people would pursue spiritual development for all the wrong reasons! I mentioned earlier that the great gurus tend to die of the same sorts of things that we do, such as conditions like cancer and heart disease. Ramana Maharshi and Ramakrishna are two of the greatest saints of our time, or of any time, and they both died of cancer. Ramana Maharshi died from cancer of the arm and Ramakrishna died of cancer of the throat. Sri Aurobindo, also one of the greatest of all saints, had prostate problems and as a result of that went into a uremic coma and died.

VE: As we close this chapter, then, I want to reiterate once again that the primary purpose of accepting the energy blessings from the stars is for spiritual evolution rather than direct physical changes.

IF: Yes, and to me the primary benefit of spiritual evolution—toward which these energies are directed—is that it gives our life meaning. And when your life has meaning, then the physical problems that you have don't weigh you down so much. Meaning comes from connection to something greater than ourselves, and that connection is forged by love. It is our hope that the Pleiadean blessing for the opening of the heart chakra can help many people to realize that love.

☆ ☆ ☆ ☆ ☆ ☆ ☆ ☆ ☆ ☆ ☆ ☆ ☆ ☆ ☆ ☆ ☆☆ ☆ ☆ ☆ ☆ ☆ ☆ ☆

Please remember to allow one week between this and the next initiation.

Chapter 8

VEGA – THE BLESSING OF COMPASSION

Commentary by Irving

Before receiving this or any of the other star initiations, it is necessary to receive the *Subtle Body Fortification Attunement* and *Anti-Glamour Initiation* as explained on pages 69-74. Like the other star initiations, you can receive this Pleiadian initiation by simply asking for it (after doing the *Subtle Body Fortification Attunement* and *Anti-Glamour Initiation*). It is recommended that you **read this chapter** before asking for and receiving this initiation. Like the other star initiations, it takes about an hour and a quarter to receive the entire initiation. Please refer to page 79 to review the star initiation process.

This initiation from Vega is for developing the quality of universal or divine compassion. Compassion is the desire to alleviate the suffering of another. It is not empathy—empathy refers to the deep sharing of another's emotion. Compassion is more active than empathy. Nor is compassion the same as pity or sorrow. Pity and sorrow draw a line between others and us; compassion unifies us with others.

As one evolves spiritually, one naturally develops the quality that has been called universal or divine compassion. This quality bears a relationship to ordinary compassion similar to the relationship that unconditional or divine love bears to ordinary love. As its name implies, universal compassion extends to all beings without exception. However, saying this gives no inkling of its beauty and power.

Universal compassion is one of the most exquisite and life-transforming of all consciousness states. If one experiences it even for a moment, one can never again be the same. Universal compassion is important not only for the development of the individual, but for the development of humanity. The Dalai Lama has said that if humanity is to survive, compassion is a necessity, not a luxury.

The Vegans teach that there are three fears we humans have that are the primary emotional blocks to experiencing greater compassion. These are the fear of emotional pain, the fear of diminishment (i.e., that feeling compassion will somehow take away something from one's self), and fear of diversion from one's own path. The truth is, that in each case, true compassion, as distinguished from pity or co-dependence, leads to exactly the opposite of what we fear.

The Vegans want to teach everyone the following exercise for releasing these fears and developing greater compassion. Therefore, this exercise is separate from their star initiation for compassion and can be done by anyone, regardless of whether they want to receive the Vegan initiation or not. The exercise should be done only when a person actually wants to develop the quality of compassion and feels that one of the three fears is blocking it. The quality of compassion cannot be forced. We should note, of course, that compassion is best developed by working with both energy and with one's consciousness as well. Imagining what it is like to be in another's place is a good practice. The exercise is based on the fact that *when any of the three fears is blocking compassion there is some closing of the solar plexus chakra that needs to be released.* The exercise has three steps and one should spend at least two to three minutes on each step.

1) Relax the solar plexus. Breathe in and out of the solar plexus to encourage it to relax.

2) Imagine that there is a flower in the solar plexus and that its petals are opening. The flower is pointing upwards towards the top of your head.

3) Let go of the image of the flower. Imagine that a tree is rooted in the solar plexus and grows upward until the top of the tree is at the center of the heart chakra. Then imagine that the top of the tree is spreading out wards in all directions until it encompasses the whole heart chakra.

This entire exercise takes less than ten minutes, and it is heartily recommended that it be practiced on a frequent basis.

The Masters who send this exercise and the blessing of the compassion initiation are from the star called Vega. Vega, the brightest star in the constellation Lyra, is about 26 light-years distant from the Earth and is about 58 times as bright as the Sun. It is the fifth brightest star in the sky, and in the Northern Hemisphere it dominates the night sky during the summer. Together with Deneb and Altair, Vega forms the "Summer Triangle." Vega was the first star to be photographed (at Harvard Observatory in 1850).

The Vegans are one of the groups who have been involved the longest with planet Earth. They work with many natural energies, including those of trees, crystals, and rocks (especially granite). Historically Vegans have played a major role in working with the Earth's energy centers and gridwork, particularly with the Earth's heart chakra. Since about 1500 A.D. they have not played as prominent a role as some other groups; however, over the next several centuries they will again come into prominence.

They are artistically oriented and have studied the creative process in great detail. Their culture prizes beauty. Vegans especially love music and are adept at using it for spiritual purposes to evoke one's "soul note." Indeed, in ancient Greece, as well as in other cultures, Vega was called "the harp star," a reference to the mythical seven-stringed lyre of Hermes. The American poet James Russell Lowell said that the strings of this lyre "give music audible to holy ears."

Vegan spirituality is similar in many ways to the Earth's tradition of Buddhism. Like Buddhism it emphasizes the development of compassion. As the quality of universal compassion develops, a subtle body we could call the compassion body, that is latent in the human energy field, begins to come forth. There is a reciprocal relationship between the evolution of this subtle body and the development of compassion. This subtle body exists at different frequency levels. As is well known, Vajrayana (one of the schools of Buddhism) has developed a number of techniques for working with these frequency levels and with this subtle body as a whole. The Vegans have developed many sophisticated light-body systems, including some which are very similar to those used in Vajrayana.

What is less well known is that as the quality of unconditional love and those states of consciousness known in the West as Christ Consciousness develop, there evolves a similar but distinct subtle body which we could call the love body. This love body is also latent in the human aura. There is a reciprocal relationship between the evolution of this subtle love body and the development of unconditional love. In the West this body has been most commonly called "the Christ body" and has been associated with esoteric Christian traditions, such as that developed by certain monks near Mount Athos. However, it is important to realize that knowledge of this body and how to utilize it belongs to no one tradition. It was worked with extensively in Kabbalah as well as by the ancient Maya and the ancient Celts.

From the perspective of the lower planes, compassion and love are related but distinct qualities. It has sometimes been said that compassion is more the desire to alleviate the suffering of another whereas love is more the desire to make another happy. From the perspective of the higher planes, compassion and love are not separate qualities, but aspects of a larger, undivided whole—different colors within the same rainbow you might say. Similarly there is an evolutionary step beyond the development of the compassion and the love body. That step is the unification of these two bodies to form a greater, undivided whole. In guiding humanity the primary long-term role of the Vegans is to help us with the unification of these two bodies. They will introduce us to specific light-body techniques to accomplish this purpose.

Conversation between Virginia and Irving

VE: Since compassion and love are so badly needed on Earth, please discuss how the Pleaidean blessing of love relates to the Vegan blessing of compassion.

IF: The qualities of love and compassion are related to each other but they are distinct qualities that are not the same. They have a different feel to them. When I talk about love and compassion I'm not talking so much about ordinary love and compassion but about divine love and compassion. However, we can sense some of this difference even with respect to ordinary love and compassion. As I said in the introductory material, compassion is generally conceived as a desire to alleviate the suffering of another, whereas love is conceived as the desire to make another person happy.

VE: How does this relate to Jesus' comments where he says love your brother as yourself or do unto others as you would have them do unto you? What is the distinction between loving another one so much that you would treat them as you would want to be treated? Doesn't that include compassion?

IF: Oh yes, certainly the two qualities are related to each other. However, if people who are reading this stop and think, and try to recreate in themselves the feeling they had when they were feeling compassion for someone and the feeling that they had when they were feeling love for someone, they will see that the qualities are not the same. Relative to each other, compassion has a more yin quality than love; love has a more yang quality than compassion. They're like two parts of a greater whole.

When one experiences really deep compassion for someone else, the sort of universal compassion that has developed in Buddhism, there is a quality of serenity or rest about it. I want to emphasize that compassion does include an impulse to action; this is the difference between compassion and just empathy. Nevertheless, there is a certain quality of stillness to deep compassion which is very hard to put into words. Relative to compassion, love has a more active quality to it.

We should not think about compassion and love in terms of one being better than the other. Rather, the development of each supports the development of the other. Most people can't go from where they are to having unconditional love for all people; they must first go through a stage of having compassion for everyone. The development of compassion for all people is facilitated by the experience of deep love for one or more individuals in our personal life.

VE: So let's bring the word peace into this discussion. Are you saying that the goal of either compassion or love has within it this universal understanding that everything is to be harmonious, mutually respected, honored and cared for?

IF: I would say that a person who has really developed Buddha Consciousness, as well as a person who has really developed Christ Consciousness, would have a feeling of peace. However, this is a quality that is more deeply developed by the Buddhist tradition. If you're around some of the Tibetan lamas, for example, they have a quality of peace or serenity which is extraordinarily strong and which radiates from their body in waves and has a very profound influence on those around them. Now a person who has pursued the path of Christ Consciousness also has a well-developed sense of peace, but the energies which radiate from them are more likely to awaken love or joy in the people who are exposed to them. There's certainly an overlap, yet they're by no means identical. It's a simplification to think that all traditions are teaching the same thing, but it's also important when we discuss their differences to keep in mind that there are important similarities. From the point of view of someone who is clairvoyant or very sensitive to energy, it's very clear that these traditions are developing different aspects of ourselves, because the energies that come from developed practitioners in these respective traditions are quite distinct from each other.

VE: Perhaps it would be a good point for you to clarify

what you meant when you said universal compassion extends to all beings without exception. Who are the beings to whom this compassion is extended?

IF: The classic phrase used in Buddhism is that compassion is extended to "all sentient beings." We're referring to those beings who have awareness, who have consciousness and who basically can suffer. The quality of suffering for animals is different than for humans because we humans have an awareness of time and we're constantly thinking about the past or the future in ways which cause us suffering. Nonetheless, if a being is developed enough to experience suffering, whether or not it's in the same form as human beings experience, then we have a moral injunction not to behave in a way which inflicts suffering upon that being.

VE: So in Hinduism, for instance, their respect for all animal forms is based on compassion for more than humans.

IF: Exactly, it includes our fellow inhabitants of the planet, and Earth herself, as well as ourselves. It even includes beings of other planets.

VE: I want to be clear that we're not holding compassion in a very restricted way. Can you explain how compassion is achieved both energetically and with one's consciousness as well?

IF: Yes, this is a very important concept. First we have to go back and look at a basic truth about the universe, which is that there's consciousness and there's energy or as some people say, vibration. The two are inextricably intertwined. You never find one without the other. It's important to realize that they are not identical, though. It's often said in the New Age movement that everything is vibration. But this simply isn't true. As human beings we have consciousness, we have free will. Things such as this cannot be purely reduced to vibrations. We have more dignity than that. We are more than simply a collection of vibrations. The phenomenal world can be said to be vibrations, but there is more to life than the phenomenal world.

One of the oldest wisdom teachings that we have, namely the Hindu tradition to which you were just referring, makes it very clear that undifferentiated consciousness does not vibrate. A distinction is drawn there between shiva (the principle of consciousness) and shakti (the principle of energy). So the idea that everything is vibration is really a New Age distortion of an ancient teaching rather than an ancient teaching itself. If we want to work with developing a quality, it's important that we work with it both from the point of view of consciousness and energy. You make much greater progress when you work with both.

The shortcoming of much of mainstream spirituality is that it totally ignores the world of energy, and thereby deprives people of a very powerful tool for their growth. The shortcoming of much of the New Age movement is that it is very focused on energy or vibration and doesn't work enough with consciousness. The primary way that we work with consciousness is through meditation. In the New Age movement I find that people don't meditate enough, and they often label things as meditation which would be more accurately called guided visualization and so forth. When I say meditation I'm talking about classical meditation, which can take many different forms such as Vipassana, mantras, or breathing processes but is distinct from such processes as guided visualizations. (See Reader's Notes for a recommended book on meditation.)

VE: Because meditation is personal silence, personal quietude...?

IF: In many cases yes, but a person can also meditate through physical movement or through sound. Whatever method is used, it is critical that it involve a process of surrender. In processes such as guided visualization, however, the intellect and the personal will are much too active. We want to transcend these things. That doesn't mean that we give them up, but they must become integrated as part of a greater whole.

VE: And speaking of that greater whole, is there any English word that really expresses the understanding that compassion and love are unified?

IF: No, I don't know of any word in English that really makes this point. I wish there were.

VE: Then what we're seeing here is a paucity of language because we haven't had sufficient interest in the subject necessary to develop the vocabulary.

IF: That's a very good point. English is quite underdeveloped with respect to distinguishing different emotional and mental states. So this creates a wonderful opportunity for people skilled with language to coin some new words or phrases.

VE: Now let's return to talking about the Vegans and the fact that they were able to hold the unification of love and compassion. What contributed to their reaching this high level of evolution?

IF: The evolutionary path that cultures on different planets take is very, very much influenced by the Solar Logos of the particular system they're in. The inhabitants of every solar system are being guided in their physical and spiritual evolution by a spiritual being, called the Solar Logos, which is using the sun (star) of that system to manifest on the physical plane—much as we are souls manifesting on the physical plane through our bodies. There's subtle energy that is coming from the Solar Logos and the ray structure of that energy influences the evolution of the particular system that it's in. The Vegan Solar Logos has a considerable Second Ray energy as well as energy configurations which promote the development of concepts similar to Buddhism.

In other words, the Vegans were influenced by the energy of Vega and its Solar Logos to move in a direction that's similar to that of Buddhism, but the addition of the Second Ray energy made them more conscious of the quality we call love. *This concept that the inhabitants of a planet are influenced spiritually by their sun is one of great importance.* It's one that was very widely recognized in the Earth's ancient times, but it's a truth we have lost sight of in modern times. We tend to think of people who talk about the Sun as being engaged in some sort of primitive sun worship. It's important to realize that when we're talking about the spiritual influence we're not talking about the physical Sun but about what has been called "the sun behind the sun." Just as we are immortal souls who are 'focalizing' on the physical plane through a physical body, the Solar Logos is a spiritual being who is 'focalizing' on the physical plane through the physical Sun.

VE: So you're saying that beyond what we see physically there is an extraordinary number of different beings of such power, compassion, and love that it's very difficult for us to imagine them.

IF: Yes, yes! It's extraordinary when you look up at the sky and realize that every star that you see is a sun and that behind every sun there is a great spiritual being. To give you an idea of the power and the level of development of our own Solar Logos, it is putting out as much energy on the higher spiritual planes as the physical Sun is putting out on the physical plane. We are talking about beings of such development and such spiritual luminosity that it's difficult for the human mind to conceive of these beings.

VE: It really boggles the imagination. But intrinsically we know it's true because there's this deep sense of resonance with those thoughts.

IF: We're starting to see a re-awakening in modern times, a glimmer which will grow into a fire, of the awareness of the importance of the Solar Logos.

VE: You were talking earlier about the Vegans and how they can affect the Earth. How is it that from such a distance they are able to use their energies to affect trees, rocks, and crystals? It sounds like focused attention to the mineral kingdom. Can you say why the minerals and plants need this attention rather than the Vegans just focusing on what we think of as the most important aspect—humanity?

IF: The first point to realize is that there's more to rocks and plants than meets the eye. Each rock and each plant is putting out an energy. All of these energies that the different kingdoms of nature are putting out are interrelated to each other. We can think of the world as a living mandala. Each plant, each animal, each mineral, each human being is a part of that mandala. For example, the energies which plants and minerals emit have effects on people, and from a larger perspective, each rock and each plant has a role to play in our co-evolution. Many times the masters, who are part of a civilization working with the Earth, can help to accelerate that evolution by speeding up the evolutionary process of different plant and rock groups. Sometimes the reason that they work with particular plants or rocks has to do with the fact that the rocks or plants are similar to ones that exist on their own world. Sometimes it has more to do with the future of that rock or plant. In other words, the energies that an Earth rock or plant needs as part of its evolution are similar to ones which that particular group of masters is expert at working on.

VE: Is there a reason you haven't mentioned the animal and bird kingdom in relation to Vega? Is there a particular star group that we have mentioned previously, or will be mentioning, that have relationships specifically with what we call either wild animals or domestic animals?

IF: Different groups of masters are helping to send energies to various animal species as well. The reason I'm talking more about plants and rocks is that it's easier for them to have a more immediate impact on human evolution since it's easier for a plant or mineral matrix to hold certain kinds of energies and also to hold a wider variety of energies. There's a much wider variety of energies that a rock can hold without violating the integrity of the rock than you could send to an animal without having an adverse effect on it. Also, human civilizations are located mostly on solid ground or rock.

VE: So the physical location for most of us requires proximity to the soil and a mineral base.

IF: That's right. Everyone on the planet is exposed to some sort of radiatory influence from the mineral kingdom whereas not all are exposed to the animal kingdom. In larger cities, except for our pets, people are mostly isolated from the animal kingdom.

VE: In speaking about the mineral kingdom, crystals have been utilized in past history and even presently as a conductor and/or transmitter. People know that crystals are a very powerful living material that they can program and utilize for healing and other purposes, including computers and technological devices.

IF: The more developed a crystalline structure a mineral has, the more it can hold and amplify energy. Also when masters send energy to a rock in a particular location that energy can be extended to all rocks of the same kind around the planet more easily than energy sent to a particular animal can be extended to all other animals of the same kind.

VE: One of the most important things that you have mentioned in this chapter has to do with the Vegan desire to help us clarify our fears, help us understand how fears affect us, and to offer specific assistance. So I'd like to discuss that topic more fully. You mentioned three fears: the fear of pain, the fear of being diminished somehow by giving compassion to other people, and the fear of diversion from your own path because you're busy working to help the other sentient beings. How do these fears relate to material in A Course in Miracles, which said there are only two choices: the choice of love or fear. Will you clarify or discuss that belief for us?

IF: I think if we take the statement that there are only two choices—love or fear—and substitute the word compassion for love, then it would be equally true. Fear is one of the most potent forces that is keeping us from evolving and moving along our spiritual path. These many fears include those we're aware of as well as the fears that we're not conscious of. *Our challenge is to become aware of those fears that are unconscious.* We can do this through various forms of personal growth. Many classical spiritual teachers discourage personal growth or therapy saying that it's coddling the ego, coddling the personality, and that we should transcend the personality. My perspective is just the opposite. Personal growth and spiritual growth are inextricably intertwined. You can only go so far along the path of personal growth without evolving spiritually and you can only evolve so far spiritually without evolving personally. So the more that we can understand how our unconscious fears limit us, the more we are able to grow personally and spiritually into both love and compassion.

VE: Of the three fears you mentioned, most people know about pain and suffering and their fear of them. But the fear of diminishment seems unique. Do you want to say more about that?

IF: When I refer to fear of diminishment I mean a fear which often is not completely articulated by the person who is experiencing it. Their fear is that by showing compassion they will somehow lose out and take away something from themselves. An obvious example of this loss is time and money. People might fear that if they get involved in a certain cause that they're not going to have time to do something else that they wanted to do, or if they donate to a certain charity they fear that they're going to reduce their own finances. It also includes a more psychological fear which is the fear of being taken out of oneself; the fear that one will be co-opted by something external. This is starting to bridge more into the third fear, which is fear of being diverted from one's path by too much concern for others.

VE: So is there any difference between the way a Buddhist might relate to these three fears and the way a Christian might relate to them?

IF: A person pursuing a Buddhist path and a person pursuing the Christian path would have pretty much the same human fears. We also fear experiencing universal love for similar reasons to those outlined for fearing universal compassion. I think that it's important for a person to realize that either case—being more compassionate or being more loving—does not involve being a doormat. When one is compassionate or loving towards all beings, that includes one's self. That's the difference between experiencing universal love, or universal compassion and co-dependence. People who are truly loving or truly compassionate to themselves, don't allow certain things to happen to themselves. I think the source of many of these fears is our childhood upbringing in which we learned to sacrifice our authentic self for the false self our parents and our culture fostered on us.

VE: So we're not saying that compassion and love are totally separate from each other, but rather the ideal is to hold both in some greater context into which we're evolving.

IF: Yes, and it's also important to realize that Buddhism includes love and Christianity includes compassion. The deeper reality that we're talking about is the energetic reality. When a person experiences universal compassion or divine compassion there are certain energy changes which take place in their energy field. Similarly, when a person experiences love, by which I mean universal love or divine love, there are also vibrational changes which take place in their energy field. While these changes are related to each other, they are by no means identical. The crucial point to understand is that these energetic changes complement each other and are part of a greater whole.

VE: And we have no way to describe these energy realities in words?

IF: True. We have neither the words nor the tradition that has evolved an energy practice that works with this larger picture. We have a very well-developed tradition in Buddhism that works with certain frequencies and develops what we might call, for lack of a better term, the compassion body. (The Buddhists have a very technical language that I won't bother to go into here to describe all of this.) In the esoteric Christian tradition we have techniques for developing what might be called the love body, but these techniques have been essentially lost in modern Western society. The development of the compassion body is a part of mainstream Buddhism, but the development of the love body is not at all a part of mainstream Christianity! So for humanity to evolve a fully developed subtle body field, which integrates both the love body and the compassion body, knowledge of how to develop each body separately must become more widespread—then we can work on the integration of the two. It's in this area that the Vegans will be of great benefit to humanity. As time goes on they will be teaching us specific techniques for doing this. But first we have to do our part and spread these Buddhist techniques much more widely and do the same for the Christian techniques, which still exist only in esoteric circles. Both must become much more mainstream.

VE: You mentioned earlier that the Vegans were working with the Earth's energy centers and gridwork until about 1500 A.D. It's my understanding that the Earth grid is presently expanding and shifting and having quite an upgrade. If the Vegans pulled back from being involved in that, who's doing that now?

IF: When I said that the Vegans hadn't played as prominent a current role as before, I meant that they are still continuing to work with us; it's just that other groups are more involved now. One group, which is currently playing a particularly prominent role, is the Pleiadeans, and we can see a growing awareness in the New Age movement about their importance. Much of this just has to do with the way the shifting energy structure of the Earth's gridwork manifests over time. It wasn't preordained that in 1500 A.D. the Vegans would stop working as much as they had been. That just happens to be the time when they were able to accomplish their immediate objective.

VE: It's like there's a team at work and whoever is able to do the best at the moment moves forward if they've made that commitment.

IF: That's exactly right. Humanity is part of a much larger fabric than it realizes. We're being helped by more sources than is commonly realized, and which one is helping us at a particular moment is partly the result of plans which have been in existence for millennia, and partly just the result of how things happen to fall out at that moment in time. I want to emphasize that most of the changes to the Earth's gridwork come from our own planetary Spiritual Hierarchy, even though we're focusing on non-terrestrial sources as the subject of this book.

VE: Since our physical and emotional reaction of fear so profoundly affects the solar plexus chakra, how can we keep it clear of that fearful reaction? How can people determine if these energies from Vega are helping them release their fears?

IF: One of the best ways to release fear—aside from any effects that might come from these various star initiations—is to work with shakti or an intelligent spiritual energy; such as the Drisana system or the Huna system that the S.U.N. organization teaches (or the systems made available by other groups).

The way one really determines the usefulness of anything is by the effects that one sees in one's life. Jesus said, "Judge a tree by the fruit it bears." However, I encourage people who are doing these initiations to keep logs of changes that they see in their lives because it's very, very easy to become acclimated to a new level of being. One way that we see this in ordinary life is that people who have a chronic pain that subsides, often won't even remember the moment when it disappeared. They became acclimated very quickly to the new level of health and well being.

VE: Even though we're focusing at the solar plexus chakra as a primary influence, we must understand that fear is totally pervasive in the human system almost immediately upon thought.

IF: Right. That's one of the reasons why it's so useful to work with shakti because as human beings we will have certain preconceptions. We might think, "I'm feeling fearful and so I need to clear my solar plexus" and consequently not work on other areas which are equally or even more important. On the other hand, a shakti comes into the energy field without any preconceptions and begins to work on whatever needs attention.

VE: In the introductory material you described an exercise from the Vegans for clearing fear of compassion from the solar plexus. Do we have to do some inner cleansing before that exercise can help us?

IF: Not if you have the willingness to change. You don't have to wait to do that exercise or to start on the initiation program in this book. However, it is true with all of the star initiations (and the *Anti-Glamour Initiation*) that by working on ourselves *after* we receive the initiation, we can augment the power of the initiation. It's even more helpful with the Vegan initiation, than with some of the other initiations, for us to do our own clearing. The exercise given at the beginning of this chapter helps the Vegan initiation be more easily and deeply integrated because the frequencies of that initiation are particularly responsive to visualization.

VE: Since this particular exercise for clearing the fear of compassion is so useful, how often should we do it?

IF: There's not really any set rule because *the exercise should be done at the moment a person is actually experiencing one of these fears.* How often you do the exercise depends on how often you fear experiencing compassion.

VE: But it would be advisable to simply run through it until you knew it so well you could recall it during a moment of fear, right?

IF: Let's put it like this; you can't overdo this exercise. A person can do this as often as desired.

VE: Then it's important for readers of this chapter to realize they have some extra homework if they want to make this initiatory experience more profound, longer lasting, and more useful.

IF: Yes, and it's generally true that the more individuals work consciously to develop the qualities that the various initiations are meant to instill, the more progress they will make. Energy work is so powerful and so transformative that people can lose sight of the fact that they must also do their part. In developing compassion, for example, it is also very useful to recognize when we are in judgment of someone or something. Judgment separates us from others and is opposed to compassion, which unifies us with others.

VE: So we must come to the realization that whether we have been following a particular philosophical or religious belief that teaches this information or not—it's time to utilize both what we call compassion and love. The underlying intention is to help us tap into the broader source of life from which these energies flow.

IF: That's well said and one of the things that we find in all the esoteric traditions is the understanding that spiritual qualities can be developed and unified through energy work. This is what is so sadly missing in mainstream Western religion. What you can accomplish with energy work in terms of personal and spiritual transformation is quite extraordinary. In fact, what I have found is that even most people who do energy work professionally don't really know the full limits of how much can be accomplished. That's because most people have only been exposed to the energies which are the most commonly available and not to those which are the most powerful.

VE: Going back to the earlier subject of why the Vegans are putting certain energies into the Earth's gridwork and why they are working with the Earth's heart chakra in particular, is there anything else you'd like to say?

IF: I want to emphasize again the reciprocal relationship between human evolution and the evolution of the Earth's gridwork. As the Vegans and other groups put certain energies into the Earth's gridwork and particularly into the Earth's heart chakra, it helps the evolution of the human heart. It helps us to evolve to a place where we are more in touch with universal love and universal compassion and where our subtle energy bodies are changing beyond where they are today. As we develop more love and compassion we will take better physical care of the Earth, and we will be putting out energies which in turn facilitate the development of the Earth's energy system. Eventually, small groups of people and then increasingly larger groups will bond together and, under spiritual guidance, will consciously place certain energies into the Earth's gridwork and into the Earth's heart chakra.

VE: Isn't it wonderful to remember that where energies are concerned, a human being can be both a receiver and emitter of these blessings? These blessings may be passed by a look, a touch, and of course through the physical coming together where two or more are gathered in consciousness. Whenever that gathering goes beyond the purely personal into the greater group consciousness, that joining further empowers all of life including the planet…thus moving humanity along its spiral of evolution.

IF: I so agree! The people who read this book and who receive these initiations have the opportunity to be pioneers and to play a major role in that evolutionary process. Those who receive these energies are not just helping themselves but by simply being in the presence of other people and planet Earth, are emitting frequencies which are facilitating our movement along that evolutionary spiral.

☆ ☆ ☆ ☆ ☆ ☆ ☆ ☆ ☆ ☆ ☆ ☆ ☆ ☆ ☆ ☆☆ ☆ ☆ ☆ ☆ ☆ ☆ ☆
Please remember to allow one week between this and the next initiation.

Chapter 9

BETELGEUSE – THE BLESSING
OF EXPANDED SOUL AWARENESS

Commentary by Irving

Before receiving this or any of the other star initiations, it is necessary to receive the *Subtle Body Fortification Attunement* and *Anti-Glamour Initiation* as explained on pages 69-74. Like the other star initiations, you can receive this initiation from Betelgeuse by simply asking for it (after doing the *Subtle Body Fortification Attunement* and *Anti-Glamour Initiation*). It is recommended that you **read this chapter** before asking for and receiving this initiation. Like the other star initiations, it takes about an hour and a quarter to receive the entire initiation. Please refer to page 79 to review the star initiation process.

The purpose of this Betelgeuse (pronounced 'bee-tuhl-jooz, and sometimes spelled Betelgeux) initiation is to increase your awareness of your soul. The Pleiadean and Vegan initiations have prepared the way for this initiation. The opening of the heart chakra in the Pleiadean initiation facilitates the inflow of love. The inflow of compassion in the Vegan initiation facilitates awareness of the soul, because the true source of compassion is the soul. The soul cannot be defined in words, although it can be experienced. There are three primary aspects of the soul: *will, love, and higher mind*. This initiation works with the love aspect of the soul, whereas the Pleiadean initiation affects the personality level. Some people, while receiving this Betelgeuse initiation, or in the weeks afterwards, may temporarily feel as though their body were dissolving and they were becoming pure love. They may also temporarily have the feeling of being drawn upward and being ungrounded. Do not be afraid if these feelings happen to you— they are normal and sensations of bodily awareness and groundedness will return as the soul energy is integrated during the initiation process. In order to make a quantum jump in one's level of soul awareness, it is actually necessary to go through a temporary phase of being ungrounded.

The masters from Betelgeuse teach us: "Understand who you are. You are the marriage of soul and flesh. Without the soul the body is lifeless clay; without the body the soul is a flower without earth. The soul is divine movement; the soul is God in motion. Wherever there is movement, there is soul. The soul is the movement, the body is what moves."

The holy teaching regarding the union of body and soul is given on all planets, and there arises resistance to these teachings on all planets. Resistance comes from two different camps—those who wish to be only a body and those who wish to be only a soul.

Soul awareness comes in stages or phases, not all at once. In each new stage of increased soul awareness there is a strong infusion of soul energy into the personality. During such stages one can easily make the mistake of thinking one is only a soul. Some people become stuck in this phase. The next phase is one in which the soul energy is integrated into one's physical form. This alternation of emphasis between one's spiritual aspect and one's form aspect occurs for all beings, even those whose form aspect is already a body of light rather than a dense physical body. The reason so many spiritual teachings emphasize the soul is that most people are greatly over-identified with their physical form and need to move into the phase of soul identification. The reason we emphasize the cyclical alternation of focus on spirit and physical form is that the initiations offered to you in this book have the power, over the course of a number of years, to take you through several cycles of this seesaw process. It is important to realize that neither the initiations in this book nor initiation in general is a romantic escape from the realm of form but rather is a means through which one can render greater service within the realm of form. D.K. tells the disciple that initiation "involves no leaving of the former field of activity in which he has worked and lived..." (The Rays and the Initiations, p. 539).

The masters who bring you this initiation are associated with Betelgeuse, a yellow-orange supergiant about 540 light-years from the Earth. Betelgeuse is one of the largest known stars. It is the brightest star in the constellation Orion and the eleventh brightest star in the night sky. Its volume is at least 160 million times that of our Sun, but remarkably its mass is only about 20 times that of our Sun.

Orion, the brightest of the constellations presently known to humanity, has been associated since ancient times with awareness of the soul. In ancient Egypt, for example, this association occurred through the figure of Osiris. The energies of the stars within the constellation Orion complement each other particularly well, as we'll see in the next initiation using the Rigel energies, which also come from the Orion constellation. The masters from various stars in the Orion group are expert at helping humanity with the whole process of "personality-soul fusion," but each star also has a particular specialty. The specialties of the masters from Betelgeuse include helping people experience the love aspect of the soul, integrating soul and body, and releasing the fears that often accompany the influx of a large amount of soul energy. In addition to working with the process of personality-soul fusion, the masters from Betelgeuse are especially adept at working with the metaphysical water element and the emotions. Energies from Betelgeuse are particularly useful for releasing the emotion of fear from the first chakra, including the fear of "the death of the ego" which arises during the process of personality-soul fusion.

The part of the Earth's gridwork system that the masters from Betelgeuse are most involved with is the part below Earth's waters. For most people the phrase "Earth's gridwork system" conjures up images of land masses, but remember that most of the Earth's surface is under water. The primary work of the masters from Betelgeuse is yet to occur. It will happen at a time when many more people on the Earth have become soul-infused personalities

Conversation Between Virginia and Irving

VE: What's your understanding of the soul, and how can we increase our awareness of it?

IF: I don't believe it's possible to convey in words a really good understanding of the soul because the soul must be experienced to be understood. However, one of the more successful attempts to define the soul is the classic statement that the soul is neither matter nor spirit, but the intermediary between the two. We can find that statement in many writings, from ancient times down to the present. In modern times we can find it in the works of the psychologist James Hillman and in the teachings of D.K. in the Alice Bailey writings.

There are many misconceptions about the soul. There are so many misconceptions that, in my work with people, I've found it's almost more important to explain the misconceptions about the soul than to try to explain everything the soul is. Many of these misconceptions come from not appreciating that the soul is the intermediary between spirit and matter and involve thinking of the soul as either too much like spirit or thinking of the soul as too much like matter or the personality.

We are thinking of the soul as too much like spirit if we think of it as something that we won't meet until we die, something that has no relevance to our daily life. The truth is that the soul is a living reality that we are meant to experience here on Earth, thereby bringing feelings of profound joy, aliveness and love into our daily life. I believe that most people have such experiences partially; however, fuller experiences can be fostered through openness, meditation, and energy work. We are thinking of the soul as too much like the personality when we project our negativity onto it and describe it as making wrong choices, moving away from God, etc. The truth is that the soul is in profound union with God, is completely pure, and has no moral lessons to learn. The reason it is so important to see through all these misconceptions is that they result in our experiencing our own thought forms about the soul rather than the soul itself.

VE: You said earlier that out of the three aspects of the soul (*will, love,* and *higher mind*) we can most easily experience the love aspect of the soul. Since you say that this Betelgeuse initiation works primarily with the love aspect of the soul, what happens to the aspects of will and higher mind, which we have not previously discussed?

IF: Because the seven initiations together develop all aspects of Christ Consciousness, they do include will and higher mind. In this Betelgeuse initiation we're focusing primarily on the love aspect of the soul because that is the way most people can experience their soul's influences. Let's put it like this: it's much more common for people to connect to the soul through love and through compassion than it is through the will and higher mind. I would say that the most common experiences people have of their soul is when they feel like they're being touched by something of great importance, something that transcends ordinary life—and this comes through love.

I would say the next most common way that people experience the soul is through divine beauty. Let me give you an example of what I mean by each type of experience. There are times in our life when we feel an overwhelming love that seems to be coming from something greater than ourselves and not just the personality. In some of these cases it's obvious that the source isn't the personality because of the magnitude of that love and because it suddenly comes upon us at a moment when we might otherwise feel a negative emotion towards someone. We might be angry at them, and then out of nowhere we suddenly feel our common bond of humanity with that person. We feel compassion or even love for them. So it's clear that the feeling is not just coming from our everyday personality. An example of a person being touched by beauty could come from certain scenes in nature, like watching a sunset or appreciating trees or flowers. Listening to music can also touch us profoundly. The kinds of experiences I'm talking about are not simply feeling pleasure or aesthetic enjoyment, but realizing that the beautiful sunset or the music is pointing to something beyond it, something that is greater. So we have a very profound experience of feeling something that is extraordinarily beautiful and meaningful and quite beyond our personality. The beauty in nature or any artistic beauty is a remembrance of the soul.

VE: How do these differences between love, will, and higher mind manifest in our daily life?

IF: Love, will and higher mind are distinguishable but interrelated aspects of the soul. A person could be very well-developed along one of these lines but not along the other. Some people are very tuned-in to higher mind, but not to love. It's necessary to distinguish between lower mind and higher mind. Lower mind reasons, works with data, draws analogies, etc., in order to reach conclusions. *Higher mind knows just by knowing.* When we experience higher mind we're connected to the universe. Some people use the term "cosmic mind" to express this interconnectedness with the universe. As I was saying, I know people who mentally understand the laws, yet they really don't have that much love and compassion. So it's possible to have one aspect developed without developing the other aspects. However, the development of any one aspect, if pursued far enough and with enough openness, can eventually lead to the development of the other aspects. Most people find it's easiest to tap into the love aspect of the soul, which in turn helps to develop the other aspects.

For example, the development of love can lead to the development of will. The concept of divine will and surrender to divine will is a very unpleasant concept for many Westerners. Now if you had to summarize the spiritual path in one word, that word would be *surrender*. A friend of mine told me a joke which goes, "Red light = stop; green light = go; white light = surrender." But in the West we tend to associate surrender with subjugation, or even with slavery. That's because in the West many of us have a very distorted image of God as an old man up in the sky who watches everything we do and doesn't approve of most of it. On the other hand, the Eastern traditions emphasize more the immanent aspect of God, the aspect of God that is the deepest part within our own being.

You will resist surrender as long as your personality is projecting your problems with authority issues, including the parental authority that we experienced when we were growing up, onto God. It's only when you realize that you are not surrendering to an external authority, not just surrendering to rules, but surrendering to your own deepest self that you can surrender to divine will. The paradox is that through surrender we become freed to be our true selves. In fact, it is *only* through surrender that we can become our true selves.

VE: I suppose we are psychologically attached to the idea that surrender follows defeat in a war, a battle, or confrontation. It means being demeaned or beaten somehow. We refer to ourselves and others as "losers." So I'm always seeking a way to clarify that this surrender process is helping us to acquire vast portions of ourselves that are otherwise lost— locked away by our own doing. It's like the prodigal son returning home. Surrender is gain, not loss, for the evolving personality.

IF: Agreed…now let me conclude my thought about how experiencing love helps us to tune-in to higher will. When we experience the all-embracing and very beautiful love, the infinite love, which God is always feeling or emanating—that makes it easier for us to experience divine will. Now, of course, I'm speaking in generalizations, and these things are different for different people. Some people find it easier to experience the will aspect of God than the love aspect.

VE: Let me share an aside here. In <u>A Course in Miracles</u> there is great emphasis about willingness. Willingness implies a cooperation; it implies an association with spirit which helps us to use our free will as a gift to ourselves.

IF: I certainly would agree with those comments about willingness. In fact, the energies of the Betelgeuse initiation make it easier to be willing to surrender to the soul's influence.

VE: I liked that comment from the Betelgeuse masters saying that we are the marriage of soul and flesh...that without the soul the body is lifeless clay; without the body the soul is a flower without earth. So why is it that we humans aren't living that marriage of soul and flesh?

IF: It's because the soul can be masked by the imperfection of the personality. It's very important to understand that the soul is completely pure and is completely in union with God. This is something that we find stated over and over again in the great mystical teachings. There's a famous Kabbalistic prayer that thanks God for the purity of the soul. In the Hindu understanding, it's stated quite clearly in the Upanishads that *the soul is pure.*

In the modern West we have corrupted these teachings, and people talk about the soul as making wrong choices or moving away from God. It's very important to realize this is impossible, that the soul is always totally in union with the will of God. It's the personality that makes wrong decisions by moving away from God. There's a very beautiful analogy which one finds in many Eastern traditions and also in the West. It describes a person as being like a lamp whose glass is encrusted over with dirt leaving the interior light pure and uncorrupted. The dirty glass that covers up the light represents all the imperfections, the impurities, the distortions of the personality. Our job is to clear away the dirt, so that the light that was always there can shine through. What we call evil is the interference of the personality with the pure, uncorrupted nature of the soul. Evil is simply the absence of good. From a higher perspective, *evil is good which hasn't arrived.* To use a physical analogy, there is a particle of light, namely a photon, but there is no particle of blackness. If a room is dark it's not because there's something called a "black on" being emitted; it's because there's an absence of light.

VE: Right. Now I'd like to talk more about what this initiation does to a person's body. Does the energy enter the heart chakra or does it enter the entire auric system?

IF: In terms of the underlying energy dynamics, this initiation affects all the chakras. However, it is true that it focuses on the heart chakra because that is the chakra which is most directly connected with the experience of love.

VE: So you say that if people feel temporarily as though their physical body is dissolving and they are becoming pure love, they should not be alarmed by that feeling and simply know that's normal. Similarly, those feelings of being ungrounded and perhaps of being drawn upward into a higher frequency should not be worrisome?

IF: Yes, it will pass! It's part of the normal process that occurs when there is a large influx of soul energy. I'm not saying that there's always a feeling like you might dissolve into pure love, but that there's an orientation towards the higher planes which temporarily results in our being less grounded and less connected to the world of ordinary life. But of course when that energy is integrated, we're able to express that love in ordinary life. To use the analogy of a painting, love has to be expressed in the brush strokes of our life.

VE: So a person may need a little hand-holding or counseling or support as they go through these initiations?

IF: They may. It's important for people to understand that in doing any of these initiations they may have very unusual experiences. The energies can be unsettling to the defense mechanisms of the personality and therefore can be experienced as unpleasant. The point is that these experiences do not go on forever!

VE: Obviously, since we're not doctors and are not giving medical advice, each person must accept the responsibility for invoking the energy if they wish it and then be responsible for the experience they may have.

IF: Yes, and it's conceivable that someone, just by coincidence, might have some health problem that was going to manifest anyway, and it manifests right at the time that they were receiving the initiation. While these initiations in themselves will not cause health problems, nonetheless, if during the time you're receiving the initiations you have some sort of health problem, you should respond the same way you would if you weren't receiving the initiations, namely consult a licensed health practitioner.

VE: Since soul awareness comes in stages, not all at once, people should be aware that on the road to spiritual integration they can have unusual sensations from time to time.

IF: Certainly. From an energetic perspective these initiations will raise a person's vibrational rate, and it takes a certain amount of time for the energies to become grounded and integrated throughout their etheric, emotional, and mental bodies.

VE: How do we know when this has happened?

IF: You know by the difference the energies are making in your daily life, and in particular what difference they are making in terms of your ability to experience and to express love and compassion for your fellow human beings. There's a wonderful passage in the New Testament in the first epistle of John which says that he who says he is in the light and hates his brother is in the darkness still. He who loves his brother abides in the light...

The bottom line always comes back to our daily life. There are many metaphysical, abstract concepts available through which we can understand the structure of reality, but that doesn't automatically guarantee that you are becoming a better person for it.

VE: Often in the Buddhic materials there's a focus on giving service to all sentient life, not only humans, but all life on planet Earth. How does compassion toward ourselves relate to this concept?

IF: Perhaps the best way to talk about this is to say that when we develop universal compassion it is for all living beings, including ourselves. You see, that is where loving self-interest comes in. Being compassionate towards everyone doesn't mean you become a doormat and let people take advantage of you. This is actually a point that gets sticky for some followers of Buddhist teachings—those who haven't learned to distinguish between universal compassion and co-dependence. They're not the same thing. If we're truly experiencing universal compassion, then that includes compassion towards ourselves, which means we don't let other people take advantage of us.

VE: Still, with all this emphasis on showing love and compassion to other people, how can we be sure to also take care of our own needs during physical life?

IF: Good question. Just let me point out that the people who have become great spiritual leaders (ones we seek to emulate—such as the Buddha and Jesus) are people who devoted their entire life to service. These people serve as a model for us, yet at the same time we have to realize that their lives are not typical of an average human being. The reason that we know about these people, and that we're trying to emulate them in the first place, is because they were at one extreme end of a continuum. So in following them it can be easy to lose sight of one's personal needs. Of course to a certain degree it's subjective. Where do you draw the line between working for other people and taking care of yourself? One thing that I would encourage anyone to look at is this: if loving someone else is hurting you, then it's time to stop and take a serious look at what you're doing.

VE: I don't want our readers to think that we're promoting the reception of these external energies from spiritual star masters so they'll become perfected beings with 100 percent commitment to service. Our intention is that the initiations will assist each person to become a fuller expression of their divine nature at whatever pace they choose.

IF: I agree completely, and I might also add that you don't have to go out and save the world in order to become a better person or have a positive effect on the people around you. There's that wonderful book, Random Acts of Kindness, which has many examples of small things to do, such as paying the bridge toll for the person behind you, that are quite wonderful and don't involve a large expenditure of personal energy or time or involve a threat to one's well-being.

VE: Shifting back to the constellation of Orion, I wanted to talk about ancient Egypt since you had mentioned the word, Osiris. In my previous book with Tom Kenyon called <u>The Hathor Material: Messages from an Ascended Civilization</u>, we learned about a whole civilization of beings who ascended to a level of consciousness which shifted them from physical human form into a higher frequency using love and sound. These Hathors greatly influenced ancient Egypt and Tibet and were probably considered to be Egyptian gods and goddesses; yet their present message clearly relates to Christ Consciousness. Any comments?

IF: Although it's not always commonly realized or put in those terms, the ancient Egyptian mystery schools were working with the development of Christ Consciousness. It's important to realize that although on our planet Jesus was the foremost exemplar of Christ Consciousness, Christ Consciousness was not invented on the Earth. In other parts of this book we talk about the relationship between Christ Consciousness and Sirius, for example. Sirius and the stars in the constellation Orion were the two most important star groups that the ancient Egyptians worked with. In the Alice Bailey books, D.K. talks to us very explicitly about the importance of the relationship between the Christ and Sirius. Now the ancient Egyptians, under the guidance of masters from these star systems, developed to a fine art the use of energy initiations to promote Christ Consciousness.

Some readers may have seen the movie, "Stargate," in which people went through a portal and literally, physically, went to another star system. Now in my opinion that is science fiction, but what the ancient Egyptians actually did was travel in what have been called soul vehicles. They projected their soul vehicles to temples on Sirius and some of the stars in Orion, where they received initiations from the masters there. The soul vehicles then returned to their personal aura space, and the energy of the initiations was emitted slowly over time so that it was safe to absorb. In this way they were able to receive initiations of a power that would otherwise not be possible.

I've been guided today by some of these same non-terrestrial masters, who were responsible for the original initiations, to recreate an Egyptian Mystery School in which people receive initiations of this sort. The ultimate goal of all this is to reach the state of consciousness which has been described as Christ Consciousness. But again it's important to realize that this was not invented here on the Earth, and that as far as civilizations here on the Earth are concerned, no one civilization has a monopoly on it. Christ Consciousness was worked with, not just in the ancient Near East, but also by the Celts and the Mayans.

VE: So it was related to groups?

IF: Yes. Many of the initiations which were given in the ancient mystery schools, Egyptian and otherwise, are only given in groups. *Initiation is intrinsically a group process* even though from the perspective of the lower planes we might not realize this at first. We might think that we're being involved only on an individual level. On a soul level, from the perspective of the higher planes, we're already interconnected and what we're doing is embodying that connection, bringing that connection down to the lower planes.

VE: Good. Now I'd like to talk about this specialty of the spiritual masters on Betelgeuse, whose energies help people release the fear which blocks the experience of the love aspect of the soul.

IF: When there's a large influx of soul energy a person typically experiences anxiety. So first of all let me distinguish between fear and anxiety. Fear, as I use the term, is in relation to a specific, known thing. A bear might be coming at me and I experience fear as a result. Anxiety is free floating. We might be walking along and suddenly feel this anxiety without it being attached to a particular thing. Now when there is a large influx of soul energy a person might experience either or both. They might experience fear and/or anxiety. The most common pattern is for the anxiety to predominate so that the person is in a state of high tension, and they're not exactly sure why. Then the personality wants something tangible to explain its uneasiness, so the person starts thinking that they're afraid someone is going to break into their house or that they're going to die in a plane accident. The real cause of this fear is that the ego feels it is going to be destroyed.

Let me explain what I mean by ego because it's a term that's commonly misunderstood. When I talk about ego I'm not using the word in the sense that we use it when we say, "Oh that person has a big ego; they're stuck up." It's a psychodynamic structure; it's the part of you which identifies with whatever you perceive yourself to be—such as a good person, an American, a parent, etc.—and that identity takes on a life of its own.

To make this more concrete, let's say that you are watching a movie and you identify with the hero or heroine in that movie, so that when someone points a gun at the main character in the movie you feel a moment of fear. If you really look at that fear, it's the fear that you're going to be annihilated. The interesting thing is that you experience this even though you know that you're watching a movie. The reason you experience fear is that your ego has identified with that character. This is the basic nature of the ego. *The basic function of the ego is to identify.*

In real life, your ego has identified with being a particular person and being a particular body. The truth is that from a higher perspective, you are no more the bag of flesh and bones that you attach your name to than you are that character in the movie. You are, as I emphasized earlier, an embodied soul, with the emphasis here on the word "soul." You're so much greater than just the personality. When a lot of soul energy starts to come in, your ego may feel as though it's going to be destroyed.

VE: ...and that's the first chakra.

IF: It's certainly experienced in the first chakra because this is really a fear about the most basic survival of all—the survival of oneself as a being. However, one does experience it in the other chakras, like the solar plexus, as well. What we're really talking about is all the energy centers and all the subtle bodies. The reason I emphasized the first chakra is because the energies of Betelgeuse are particularly good for releasing fear from the first chakra. Now it's important to realize that the ego does not literally die, and there's a lot of misunderstanding about this. It's common to use this phrase, "death of the ego." The ego is still there even after one undergoes this process of spiritual evolution. As Krishnamurti said, "You need your ego to catch the bus." If you're going to be a separate functioning unit on the physical plane you have to have an ego. If you were so identified with being everything in the universe, not only would you miss catching the bus, but there's a good chance you're going to get run over by it. So the ego does not literally disappear or die; it becomes transformed.

The transformation is so radical, of course, that to the ego it feels as though it were going to die. If you are seriously pursuing spiritual growth, then at some point your ego will be challenged, and that will certainly be uncomfortable! That is one difference between all legitimate mystical teachings and some parts of the New Age movement which state that growth requires no pain or suffering.

VE: Let's go on to the specialties of these Betelgeuse masters. You said that not only are they able to help work through these rigidities, especially the fears of the first chakra and beyond, but also they're particularly adept at working with the water element and the emotions. Please talk more about the metaphysical symbology of the water element and the psychological process.

IF: First of all, the emotions are most closely connected to the water element. Of course, any master, by virtue of being a master, is able to work with all the elements, but the masters from Betelgeuse are particularly adept at raising the vibratory rate of the water element and providing a freer flow of positive emotions. As we were saying before, when a person becomes realized or enlightened, the ego or personality doesn't disappear. So all masters and all enlightened beings do continue to have a personality with particular specialties and inclinations. I should say again that any master can work with multiple energies and could have given any initiation offered through this book. It's just that masters, like all beings, have a set of particular, organized preferences according to their *ray structure.*

VE: Could you explain how the Betelgeuse masters use the Earth's gridwork system to affect physical water?

IF: First of all, when I use the term gridwork system I'm talking about the subtle energy network, which pervades and extends outward from the Earth. When people hear the term "Earth's gridwork," they tend to have images of solid land; however, remember that most of the planet is covered by oceans. That part of the gridwork system which is underwater is also of great importance, and it is this part with which the masters from Betelgeuse are working. What they're doing is causing the water of the oceans to become more structured or organized—like a liquid crystal. As many readers know, by virtue of its structure, a crystal can hold much information and energy. As the ability of the Earth's oceans to hold energy increases, all of the masters who are helping the Earth can better use the oceans to facilitate the evolution of the planet and of humanity. Because there is a resonance between the water in the oceans and the water in our cells, positive changes in the oceans increase the structuring of the water in our cells, enabling them to hold more information and energy.

The water in living cells is naturally different than the water that comes out of your faucet because it is more structured. What the masters from Betelgeuse are doing through their work with oceans is augmenting a natural property of water in living tissue. By affecting the subtle energy structure of the oceans and ultimately the water's physical nature, it will hold more information and energies with which we can resonate. As we will see when we get to the chapter on the Rigel initiation, the masters from Rigel are directly affecting the energy field and thereby the structure of the water in our human cells. There is an intimate relationship between the structuring of cellular water and our spiritual evolution. As we evolve spiritually, the water in our cells naturally becomes more structured. When the water in our cells becomes more structured, it enables us to hold more and higher vibrational energy, thus facilitating our spiritual evolution.

VE: Is there any difference between whether that's fresh water, such as lakes and rivers, rather than oceans and salt water?

IF: The masters are working with fresh water as well as ocean water. Regarding the salt content in ocean water, salt is an excellent holder and conductor of energy, and the salt in the oceans definitely plays a major part in this. One of the metaphysical properties of salt is that it promotes flexibility. You can see this particularly in the mental body. The primary jump that must occur for most of the human race is the jump from being focalized on the mental body to being focalized on the causal body, which is the lowest of the spiritual bodies. As D.K. puts it, "the ring pass not," for the average person is the mental body. So there's a relationship between the evolutionary process through which this happens and the salt in the oceans.

VE: Going back to the causal body you just discussed, is there a clear way to indicate whether these star initiations—and particularly this one which is coming to open the soul's love aspect—are likely to be bringing more people into that causal body experience? Is that really what we've been talking about?

IF: Absolutely. The experience of divine love or divine compassion is one that must involve the activation of the causal body. It's very important to understand that the spiritual realm—although it's interrelated to the physical, emotional, and mental realms, is a distinct realm. It's a mistake to try to reduce spiritual experiences to just physical, emotional, and mental components (which is what many people do). What I often see is that people understand the nature of spiritual experience mentally, but their causal body is not really activated. This can happen in any cultural tradition, but especially in America where many New Age people talk about being in connection with their Higher Self when what they really are in connection with is *their own thought forms of what the Higher Self should be.* Whether a person is really in touch with their Higher Self or not is very clear to someone who is clairvoyant enough because they can really see an activation in the causal body.

I would like to point out the usefulness of understanding structure and its relationship to consciousness. Many people who are more traditionally-oriented see the New Age emphasis on working with energy, chakras, and subtle bodies and wonder what all this has to do with spirituality. When you understand the intimate connection between consciousness and energy, then the question does not even arise. However, you can go too far in the other direction. We see many people in the New Age movement who are very concerned about opening their chakras, working with energy, and the development of their subtle bodies, but they're not practicing the central concerns of spirituality—love, compassion, and service to one's fellow human beings.

VE: So it's a very delicate balance with constant choice, since we have free will!

IF: It is a balance, and we do indeed have to exercise our will to work on ourselves. I would say to people who are very much into energy work that it's not enough to just run energy on yourself. You must also work with your consciousness. You can run energy on yourself 'till you're blue in the face, but you'll never become enlightened through that activity. I meet many people who think if they just have one more initiation or one more attunement they'll become enlightened. It doesn't work that way because in the final analysis running energy on yourself is just another experience. It may be an extraordinarily beautiful experience, and you may see divine white light and cosmic fireworks, etc., but in the end it's simply another experience. And *part of being enlightened is being able to stand outside of all experience.*

VE: So my understanding is that these energies we're receiving from the masters on Betelgeuse are an introduction to the future of human awareness and will have a profound role in helping us consciously achieve more soul awareness.

IF: Yes. The people who are receiving the initiations from this book are pioneers because these initiations are helping to facilitate changes in their subtle bodies, which will not happen for many centuries for the bulk of humanity. I should also add that it's very important not to develop false pride. The changes that the initiations empower us to manifest in our daily life are what is important. Are you growing in love and compassion for your fellow human beings? If you're not, then you can have all the energy in the world and it's not really serving the purpose that it was meant to serve. Here's where work with consciousness must come into the picture. We have to work on consciously developing the qualities such as love and compassion that we want to manifest.

☆ ☆ ☆ ☆ ☆ ☆ ☆ ☆ ☆ ☆ ☆ ☆ ☆ ☆ ☆ ☆☆ ☆ ☆ ☆ ☆ ☆ ☆ ☆

Please remember to allow one week between this and the next initiation.

Chapter 10

RIGEL – THE BLESSING OF THE INTEGRATION OF MATTER WITH SPIRIT

Commentary by Irving

Before receiving this or any of the other star initiations, it is necessary to receive the *Subtle Body Fortification Attunement* and *Anti-Glamour Initiation* as explained on pages 69-74. Like the other star initiations, you can receive this initiation from Rigel by simply asking for it (after doing the *Subtle Body Fortification Attunement* and *Anti-Glamour Initiation*). It is recommended that you **read this chapter** before asking for and receiving this initiation. Like the other star initiations, it takes about an hour and a quarter to receive the entire initiation. Please refer to page 79 to review the star initiation process.

The purpose of this initiation is to facilitate the integration of your material (physical) nature and your spiritual nature. This integration is important for anyone on the spiritual path, but is particularly important for those in modern Western culture who suffer greatly from the split between body and spirit. All too often they do not realize how pervasive this split is.

There are three primary ways in which this split manifests.

1) We are split when we do not realize that each of us is a sacred embodiment of God. Walt Whitman said that if anything is sacred, the human body is sacred. If everyone lived this truth then the world would no longer be plagued by war

and the exploitation of our fellow human beings. All too often, even those who are spiritually oriented fail to honor the divinity of their own bodies by depriving them of sacred sleep, having an improper diet, and leading stressful lives. If they treated a sacred shrine, church, or temple the way they treated their bodies, they would be horrified.

2) We are split when we do not realize the sacredness of our Mother the Earth and instead treat her as a thing to be manipulated. We cannot deaden our heart to our Mother without deadening our heart to life. Fortunately, this situation is in the process of ultimately changing because of the increasing inflow of Seventh Ray energy to our planet.

3) We are split when we separate sex from worship. In the sexual act we honor the divine love, divine power, and divine creativity both in ourselves and in another. In the sexual act we commingle the divine love, the divine power, and the divine creativity from within ourselves with the divinity within another. The sexual embrace mirrors the cosmic embrace of yin and yang through which the world is born anew in each moment. When society robs us of our birthright to experience sex as a sacred act, there is a deep hole inside of us, and we seek to fill that hole with exciting experiences or possessions. This robbery is also at the root of much of the violence in our society.

For the most part, Western culture does not experience the sacredness of our sexuality, whereas Eastern cultures have a history of tantric practices. In tantric practices one lover must play the yin role and the other lover must play the yang role. However, the role one plays may vary from one occasion to another. Note that we say "yin and yang" not "female and male." It is not necessary in tantric practices for the lovers to be male and female, only that a yin-yang polarity exist. From a broader perspective it certainly ill-suits those who would call themselves spiritual to cast out their gay, lesbian, or bisexual brothers or sisters from their hearts. Love has to do with what is in your heart not with the shape of your lover's genitals.

The lack of integration between matter and spirit also affects us in ways other than the three mentioned above. It leads to a lack of wholeness, which affects our entire way of being in the world. The purpose of this initiation is to begin the process of restoring this wholeness, a wholeness whose power and beauty can be experienced but cannot really be described in words. The initiation works in many ways, though it focuses on the three aspects mentioned previously.

If you wish to facilitate this initiation, aside from remaining as open and receptive as possible, the best thing you can do is to re-conceptualize the way you perceive matter and spirit. This is true even for those who already perceive the oneness of matter and spirit because as long as one is physically incarnate there is work to be done in this area! Before discussing the foundational point of this re-conceptualization, we first emphasize that the way one perceives such fundamental aspects of reality— such as space, time, matter, karma, spirit, and God—has a much more profound affect on our daily thoughts, feelings, and actions than is often realized. Furthermore, there are many cross linkages between these perceptions and their effects. A key example occurs when we are cut off from nature and primarily perceive the linear aspect of time rather than the cyclical aspect of time. This overcharges the brow chakra relative to the heart chakra. As a result, many undesirable personal and social consequences happen, including our further isolation from nature, which results in a negative feedback loop.

It is not just our consciously held conceptions that influence our daily experience of being in the world. Our unconscious beliefs also play a major role. *The unconscious mind is a powerful controller of energy and actually shapes our subtle bodies to conform to its perception of reality.* For instance, many people are unaware that there is a continuum along which everyone falls with respect to their perception of time as elastic versus inelastic or rigid. This in turn is related to whether one perceives time more as a field for creation or an externally imposed measuring rod. The more one perceives time as an externally imposed measuring rod, the more a specific kind of rigidity enters the mental body. This rigidity hinders the integration of the emotional and mental bodies.

Our beliefs, both conscious and unconscious, also influence the flow of spiritual energy. A good example is provided by the flow of kundalini energy. Scientific observation of people having kundalini experiences without any previous knowledge or preconceptions about kundalini shows that the flow of kundalini does not stop after it has risen from the base of the spine to the top of the head. Rather, it continues over the head to the front of the body and downward. This is natural because kundalini is the master integrator of matter and spirit; the upward flow takes us into the realm of the transcendental and the Divine while the downward flow helps us to incorporate this realm into our earthly life. However, those who mistakenly believe that the flow of kundalini is supposed to stop at the crown (either from having an overly transcendental view or just from having been taught this belief) will find that this belief actually causes the flow to stop at the crown.

You may well wonder how it is possible to re-conceptualize matter and spirit. The most important change to make is to understand, in an increasingly deep way, that *matter and spirit are dualities, not opposites.* The world is organized according to the principle of duality—yin and yang, day and night, hot and cold, up and down, etc. There are three levels of increasing insight in how one thinks about duality. The least skillful way is to think of them as just opposites. The next level of insight is to understand that they are complementary parts of a greater whole. The highest level of insight is to understand that ultimately duality is an illusion and reality (God) is a seamless whole.

How do these levels work with respect to the duality of female and male? The lowest level of perception is to see female and male as just opposites; this is the "battle of the sexes" mentality. The next level of insight is to realize that female and male are complementary aspects of a greater whole. This includes the realization that each needs the other. It also includes the realization that within every man there is an inner woman (what Jung called the "anima") and within every woman there is an inner man (what Jung called the "animus"). The highest level of insight is to understand that ultimately there is only God, and what we label female and male are simply different appearances of God.

In a like manner let's consider how the three levels apply to matter and spirit. The lowest level of insight is to think of matter and spirit as opposites. An example of this type of thinking is to see the soul as pure and matter as corrupt; to see the soul as trapped in the realm of matter. The next level of insight is to see that matter and spirit are complementary, that each needs the other to be complete. They might be compared to the north and south poles of a magnet, each of which cannot exist without the other. The highest level of insight is to realize that ultimately there is only God and that matter and spirit are simply God appearing in different ways. It has been said that *matter is the outer garment of God.* The master D.K., in the Alice Bailey writings, tells us that *matter is spirit made dense and that spirit is rarefied matter.*

This initiation for the integration of matter and spirit comes from masters associated with the star Rigel. It was previously thought that Betelgeuse was the brightest star in the constellation of Orion, and Rigel was the second brightest, but newer measurements show Rigel to be the brighter of the two. Rigel is about 910 light-years from us. A blazing white supergiant, Rigel is the seventh brightest star in the sky. Robert Burnham, in Burnham's Celestial Handbook, estimates that if Rigel were as near to us as Sirius it would give us about a fifth as much light as the full moon.

The masters from Rigel think very holistically and view everything in terms of process. Their language does not contain the English equivalent of nouns. Instead of a "tree" they would talk about "treeing". They can help people integrate many different dualities, not just the duality of matter and spirit.

Like the masters from Betelgeuse, the masters from Rigel

have a deep understanding of the water element. Their particular specialty is facilitating the evolution of the energy field of the water in our *cells* rather than working with the water in the oceans. In this regard they are utilizing a little known but highly significant metaphysical power of water, namely the ability to take the Second Ray energy of Love/Wisdom as it comes from the higher planes and integrate it into our physical bodies. Understand that *because our blood is mostly water, it is a delivery system for energies of divine love throughout our body.* The masters from Betelgeuse and the masters from Rigel cooperate in a very intimate way to actualize the power of the water element for the planet and humanity's evolution.

Conversation between Virginia and Irving

VE: You've just mentioned the Seventh and Second Ray energies as being vital to humanity's evolution. Will you explain more about the rays?

IF: The first thing to say about the rays is that they are the Seven Rays of Creation, the energies out of which everything in the phenomenal world is ultimately composed. The second thing is that all of evolution can be looked at as a shifting pattern of ray energy. The entire universe is like a giant kaleidoscope of ray energies where the patterns being formed by their interaction is constantly shifting and changing. All the rays are present at all times, but at different periods in history different ray energies dominate. Although the entire Earth and humanity is on the Second Ray of Love/Wisdom, the ray that is influencing our evolution the most right now is the Seventh Ray. (See **Appendix A** for a brief description of the Seven Rays.)

D.K. tells us that the prime cosmic function of the Seventh Ray is to bring about the marriage of matter and spirit. So we observe this effect happening on our planet now. Because of its intimate connection with matter, the Seventh Ray has been associated with the divine feminine. Many of the changes that we see in our culture today are the result of the Seventh Ray stimulating the feminine aspect of human nature. One such expression of the Seventh Ray involves nurturing ourselves and others which is why we see an increasing interest in things like holistic health. Many current social changes can be best understood in terms of an increase in Seventh Ray energy coming into the planet.

VE: So the more feminine or yin energy that you're speaking about is very significant at this time?

IF: Yes. The effect of the Seventh Ray in bringing about social change demonstrates the esoteric viewpoint. The esoteric viewpoint does not deny the existence of social forces but says they operate concurrently with deeper unseen energetic influences to assist in positive changes.

VE: Given that we have this enormous support from Seventh Ray energy, why are there still so many environmental and social problems in the world today?

IF: It's always important for those of us who are involved in the esoteric sciences to remember that the physical plane has its own dynamic. There's an old saying I like which goes, "The best prayer is one with legs on it." It's fine to be concerned about the world's problems through meditating or sending people energy, but we also need to act on the physical plane!

Some of the most important actions we need to take concern Mother Earth. We pay a very heavy price for living in an overly technological society that often dishonors life. Too often we treat the Earth as a machine instead of the source of all life. Too often we treat others and even ourselves as machines instead of living beings. Eating becomes refueling and sleeping becomes a "downtime" to be minimized instead of a sacred act. Sleep should be a time of worship and re-creation, both individually and collectively, because in our sleep we collectively create society; we determine the future.

VE: Going back to the three ways in which the split between body and spirit manifests, you said that our body and spirit are split when we separate sex from worship. You mentioned tantric practices, but many Westerners may not be familiar with tantra. Do you want to comment further?

IF: There are many misconceptions about tantra. From a superficial acquaintance with it, people might think that tantra is about exotic sex techniques, techniques for prolonging orgasm, for changing the quality of your orgasm, etc. While this is a part of tantra, one must understand that the primary purpose of tantra is a sacred one through which we hope to reach enlightenment.

Through tantric practices we're honoring the sacred sexual force in ourselves and in our partner. We need to look at sexual force in a very broad way. We need to understand that it is an aspect of the Life force, with a capital "L," and also that there is an intimate relationship between sexual energy and spiritual energy. Each one can be converted into the other because they're part of the same spectrum. We could say that both sexual energy and spiritual energy are manifestations of a greater underlying unity. And the final thing I would say is that although the Hindu tantric tradition is perhaps the one most commonly known, we find tantric traditions throughout the world.

VE: Since we're talking about sexual energy, shouldn't we comment about those who are celibate?

IF: I think that for some people it is appropriate that they be celibate during certain portions of their lives. The important thing is that their sexual energy not simply be dammed up or repressed during these periods, but that the sexual energy be free flowing and be transmuted into other energy. To use the Freudian term, it can be sublimated and become the energy of political action, the energy of caring for one's friends or family, etc. The problem comes when the energy is blocked.

VE: While we're discussing aspects of sexual energy, let's not forget androgyny.

IF: Androgyny, for those who aren't familiar with the term, refers to the balance of male and female within the same individual. Androgyny is best understood in terms of energy dynamics. Part of our evolutionary process is that men recognize and integrate their inner feminine energy and women recognize and integrate their inner male energy. As time goes on we become more balanced. However, it is important to understand that even after one becomes balanced there is still a shifting back and forth between times when the male energy dominates and times when the female energy dominates.

VE: Going back to your information about the split between our body and spirit, how can the average human reconceptualize matter and spirit?

IF: That is a good question and there's not an easy answer. It's the work of a lifetime; in fact, it's the work of many lifetimes. It is particularly difficult in a culture such as America where this split is the very basis of many of our conceptions of reality. So I think the most realistic thing is just to plunge in and get started on the process, especially if these concepts are new to you. If they're familiar to you, I encourage you to think about them more deeply than before and be open to having your experience of matter and spirit change.

VE: What are some tools to keep that overcharged brow chakra you mentioned earlier—that displaces the energy from our hearts—from dominating us as a culture or as an individual?

IF: The single most important tool for anyone is meditation and by meditation, again, I don't mean things like guided visualizations. I'm referring to classical meditation which can take many forms—Vipassana meditation, mantra meditation, special breathing processes, and so forth. On a societal level I think that one of the most useful things that we can do is to create institutions which foster the learning of meditation. If everyone in our society meditated regularly then we would be changing society at the very root. Again, I want to emphasize that when I say meditation I mean a rigorous, liberation-oriented practice not such things as guided visualization or surrounding yourself with white light.

I'm not denying the usefulness of these things. I do these things myself. I teach other people to do these things, but one can easily get into the phenomenon of what I call "wallowing in white light." Nothing replaces the hard discipline of classical meditation. In saying this, I'm not trying to be a taskmaster; it's just that I would like to see people receive the gifts brought by true meditation.

Meditation not only restructures the physical, emotional, and mental bodies—which gives you more immediate benefits—but also restructures the causal body. *Restructuring your causal body is essential to your spiritual evolution and cannot be accomplished by such methods as creative visualization.*

VE: I certainly agree and recommend that everybody should meditate to get better balance of all kinds—physical, emotional, and mental, as well as spiritual. Furthermore, since the causal body is the bridge between our personal and transpersonal identity, we would be missing the most precious evolutionary opportunity promised us by not choosing to meditate.

IF: Meditation is the master unifier. It not only unifies the conscious mind and the transpersonal mind; it also unifies our conscious and unconscious minds. This is a vital topic because our unconscious minds are always at work, and this affects our interaction not only with the ordinary world but also with the spiritual world. Our defense mechanisms do not magically turn off because we're dealing with a being that is in a body of light rather than a physical body. In other words, we project our false beliefs and negative attitudes onto our spiritual guides and onto God just as much as we project them onto one another in our daily life. Now let me give a simple example of how the unconscious works. I'm sure everyone has had the experience of talking to somebody and then having that person come back a few days later and tell you just the opposite, or a different version, of what you actually said. Of course what happened was that person heard what they wanted to hear and interpreted it their own way.

VE: So everything really is controlled by our perception.

IF: Yes. As human beings we do this to a remarkable extent—far more often than most people realize. We hear what we want to hear; we see what we want to see. How is this possible? How can someone reinterpret an actual physical sound wave? It's because the receiver of this sound transmission has an unconscious belief they want that transmission to conform with. (This belief also manifests as a holding pattern in their etheric, emotional, and mental bodies.) Furthermore, the unconscious can not only reinterpret physical sound energy, it can also distort subtle energy. You see, when someone is communicating a message to us that they want us to receive and believe, they are also sending us thought forms. These thought forms travel from the sender's subtle bodies to the receiver's subtle fields and many times the thought forms are more powerful than the verbal communication. Sometimes we've had the feeling that a person is being very convincing even though their words lack power. What happened was that we were experiencing the power of that person's thought forms. Many people are familiar with the concept that body language can express more than words can. Similarly, thought forms can express more than words and body language combined.

When we're listening to someone and they're telling us something that we don't want to consciously hear, our resistance is also occurring on an energetic level. We're actually distorting the thought forms that they're putting into our subtle bodies so that they're in conformity with our thought forms. If you're clairvoyant enough you can actually see this process. You can see thought forms with a certain resonance coming in and then the person manipulating them and actually changing the resonance.

VE: Could you describe for our readers what you see clairvoyantly during our everyday communications? Let's imagine you're looking at me and you say something that I don't like. What happens outside of my physical body in my subtle energy fields?

IF: Before I answer, let me assure you that I have an agreement with my Higher Self to never influence people energetically without their knowledge. It's part of my code of ethics to stay out of people's energy fields and I've surrendered to my Higher Self in this regard. I say this because there are people who are good at manipulating subtle energy and, if they have the wrong motives, they can actually try to control other people. However, almost all of the distortion of thought forms that takes place in daily life is done unconsciously.

To answer your question about what I would see in someone's aura when they're communicating, I'll give this hypothetical example. When John and Bill are talking and Bill doesn't want to hear what John is saying, John is not only sending out verbal communications but is also sending out certain mental thought forms. If Bill doesn't want to hear, feel, and accept John's remarks, then there are different things he can do. Since the subtle matter of thought forms has properties that are analogous to the electromagnetic properties of physical matter, the most common one is simply to put up an energy barrier or magnetically repel the thought forms. Another strategy is to break up unwanted thought forms. It's also possible to take the mental matter of a thought form, "reformat it" with one's own beliefs, and return it to the sender. When someone does this to us, we can have a feeling that something odd is happening, something beyond the verbal level. These are common patterns that I see.

VE: So are there many different kinds of things that happen at an energetic level which most people aren't aware of?

IF: Yes, and it's important to understand that everybody does these things. *All of us distort the world.* All of us are continually distorting what we hear, what we see, what we remember. I once read an interesting experiment that psychologists did regarding memory. They had people keep a diary and then after intervals of weeks and months, the psychologist asked them to recount their diary entries. What they found was that as time passed people increasingly distorted their own memories.

Some people may have had the experience of looking in an old diary only to discover that the comments described there are remembered differently. I've certainly had this happen to me. The point is that this occurs all the time—much more than most people realize! Another classic psychological experiment is one in which a picture with an unarmed black man and a white man with a knife in his hand was shown to a number of people. When those who had seen the picture were asked to describe it a significant percentage described the knife as being in the hand of the black man. All of us distort our perceptions to fit our beliefs and previous life experiences. The reason that we don't realize it is because we normally don't get feedback from the external world about the validity of our belief system.

VE: Because we can't see ourselves and others distorting energy, it's as if we've imprisoned ourselves in our beliefs but we can't perceive what we've done.

IF: That's a good way to put it. In many ways it's like an invisible prison.

VE: So how does this prison of energy affect our health? We've always said health begins with the spiritual, the mental, the emotional and then comes into the physical body.

IF: Indeed it does. And many doctors estimate that 60 percent—or more—of illness has an important psychological component. When we say that someone has a psychosomatic condition we're not denying that the person is suffering. What we're saying is that there is an emotional cause, at least in part. So I should say that I'm a very strong believer in personal growth techniques, therapy, or working with your inner child. The best thing to do is to eliminate the unconscious limitations that cause these problems. Personal growth also tremendously facilitates our spiritual growth. Indeed spiritual growth and personal growth are inextricably intertwined.

As I said earlier, our defense mechanisms don't just suddenly turn off because we're dealing with a being who is in a body of light rather than a physical body. We also project our unfinished business from our family of origin and from our society onto the spiritual realm. We project it onto our guides. We project it onto God. On a cultural level we can see in the West how we have this very patriarchal image of God, which has caused great harm to us and to other cultures. However, one of the great strengths of the West is that we are coming to an understanding of the relationship between psychological growth and spiritual growth. Many, but not all, Eastern gurus have a very low opinion of therapy and personal growth techniques. They may tell students that they're just coddling the personality when this is something that they should be transcending. My own belief is that not only is personal growth very helpful to spiritual growth, but at a certain point it becomes necessary. When we've gone as far as we can down the spiritual path without working on our "stuff," we have to stop and experience more personality integration before we can proceed any further spiritually.

VE: Then achieving better health requires that we find out where our unconscious beliefs are holding us up.

IF: Absolutely, and one of the best things that anyone who wants better health can do is to get spiritual help to see their blind spots—either through opening up to spirit in a general way or working with particular guides.

VE: I always use the word "safely" open up, because I know I have a lot of negativity to release and I don't want it all to come crashing out at the same minute.

IF: That's a good thought and everyone should feel comfortable with working through his or her negativity at the pace that they feel comfortable with. No one should feel compelled to proceed at a particular moment in time. Anyone who has seriously done personal growth exploration knows it's hard work—it's the work of a lifetime. So, from time to time we deserve a vacation just as we have a vacation from our job. We need a balance between our desire to change and just relaxing into the flow of life.

May I point out that from an energetic perspective, the most profound change is a matter of balance between the energies of fire and water? One very general classification that has been given to spiritual energy work systems is to classify them into fire traditions and into water traditions. This is admittedly a generalization but it is a useful one. Probably the most famous example of working with the fire element comes from the Hinduism kundalini, which is a "fire" that arises from the base chakra and moves up the body's central channel. In general fire traditions have proved historically to be very popular because they can produce very quick results.

On the other hand, Taoism is probably the most well known water tradition, and water traditions are just as powerful and just as effective in the long run as the ones that employ fire. Some people find fire traditions too intense and prefer the water traditions, finding them more graceful or nurturing. To be fully spiritually awakened and to be balanced, we actually need both the fire element and the water element. An example of an ancient tradition that emphasized the balance of fire and water was the ancient Egyptian tradition. A tradition in modern times, which emphasizes both water and fire, is the Hawaiian one of Huna. The Huna tradition also emphasizes that male and female are simply different aspects or appearances of God. It is because of this emphasis that S.U.N. teaches Huna courses.

VE: I find it very interesting that the masters on both Rigel and Betelgeuse, which are in the constellation of Orion, are involved with affecting the water of Earth herself and the cellular water in our bodies also. Why is there such an emphasis on water?

IF: It has to do with the fact that Earth's civilizations have far too much yang, or masculine energy. In terms of the metaphysical elements this means we have too much fire element and not enough water element. This imbalance is so strong that it is as though the Earth was in flames—yet most people are not even aware of this imbalance. The masters from both Betelgeuse and Rigel are helping to restore the influence of the metaphysical water element through its vibrational linkage with physical water. The reason that there are two sets of masters involved is that they have different specialties—those from Betelgeuse help more with the water in the oceans and those from Rigel help more with the water in our bodies' cells.

Physical water is also important because of its connection to Christ Consciousness. In the introductory material for this chapter we mentioned that one of the main metaphysical functions of water is to take the energy of the Second Ray of Love/Wisdom as it comes from the higher planes, and to integrate it into our physical bodies. Because of the intimate connection between the Second Ray and Christ Consciousness there is also an intimate connection between water and Christ Consciousness. In the Sirian chapter we will discuss how, in the future, one of the main ways that the Sirians will help humanity to achieve and amplify Christ Consciousness is through "the Sirian template." In order for any activation of this template to occur, the water in our cells must be sufficiently structured so that it can hold more Second Ray energy.

The work of all the masters is interrelated. For example, the Arcturians improve the functioning of the Earth's heart chakra. This increased functioning can then better perform its job of sending Second Ray energy throughout the Earth and its subtle energy gridwork system, much as our own heart sends Second Ray energy throughout our physical and subtle bodies. A good portion of this Second Ray energy is attracted by the water in the Earth's oceans. This allows the masters from Rigel and Betelgeuse to make use of the Second Ray to evolve both the energy field of the water in the oceans and also our cells. As the water in our cells evolves to hold more Second Ray energy, humanity will become more aware of its connection to the Earth, and more and more people will consciously help the Earth's heart chakra in ways similar to those used by the Arcturians. There are many beautiful feedback loops like this.

VE: I am interested in your earlier comments about the connection between water and love and the fact that the blood carries love throughout the body. We often think of love as an experience of our totality or as a feeling in our subtle body field. Are you saying that we are now experiencing love because of what our blood contains or are you saying this is a coming evolutionary thing?

IF: Both. This is something that's happening right now in current time and as we evolve individually, and as a species, it's going to be happening both more strongly and also in a different way. It's very important to understand the more general principle that *enlightenment is enlightenment of the whole body*. When you become enlightened it's not confined to a change in your thinking or a shift in your energy field; it's a shift in your whole body. Your brain changes, your bone marrow changes, your blood changes.

This is not just theory. There have been experiments which show advanced meditators have substances in their urine which ordinary people have in lesser amounts. What comes to mind is an experiment in which advanced meditators were shown to have much more melatonin in their urine. There are many more examples. D.K. tells us that in the future people will discover many physical changes caused by meditation that far transcend what we now know. So as we evolve spiritually we change; our physical body changes, our subtle energy fields change. This is true on an individual level and it's also true on a species level.

One of the biggest shifts that will ever happen in our body will occur when the World Teacher, or what some people in Western culture would call the Christ, appears. Just through the physical presence of the World Teacher on this planet many evolutionary changes will be triggered. *A major change is that the World Teacher's energy field will trigger connections between the left and right hemisphere of the human brain.* The hemispheres will consequently become much more integrated, not just as a neuronal pattern, but because new brain tissue—not present in humans today—will form.

VE: Can you explain how a future World Teacher relates to the present Cosmic Consortium bringing forth these seven special star energies?

IF: The World teacher is coming to help our planet evolve not in isolation and separation but in cooperation with the greater cosmic plan and spiritual community.

VE: Then you're saying that non-terrestrial beings are actually contributing to both subtle and physical body changes in human beings as part of our evolutionary process?

IF: Yes. I think the most helpful thing for people to understand about evolutionary changes today is that the greatest changes taking place for individuals are actually not physical changes at all. We should shift our focus from what's happening on the physical to what's happening for our subtle bodies. Why? Because the subtle bodies are much more elastic than the physical.

The way to change the subtle bodies, as I've said before, is through energy work and meditation. Meditation is also crucial for the development of the pineal gland, which grounds and integrates subtle energies into the physical body. Western cultures have adapted Eastern knowledge about the chakra system, but lack application of Eastern knowledge about the vital role of the glandular system. D.K. indicates that as your glands are, so are you. Many of the current difficulties that people in the New Age movement experience are present because they lack knowledge about their glands. Currently this is a far more critical issue than merely focusing concerns on the DNA.

VE: Just to conclude that thought, doesn't meditation ultimately affect physical and subtle body DNA?

IF: Of course, and ultimately the changes which are taking place in the subtle DNA will show up as changes in the physical DNA. However, that's a much longer process than most people think. When you're on a spiritual path, it's important to develop the quality of divine patience. I've seen people who are constantly pushing themselves to bring in higher and higher energies, but they're going too fast and their physical body is paying the price for that.

VE: What you're saying emphasizes once again that one of the hardest human lessons is being willing to appreciate our physical life because it raises seemingly unanswerable questions such as "Who am I?" and "Why am I here?"

IF: These are some of the biggest questions that anyone can ask. Why are we all here in the first place? I think an answer to that question may be one that the human mind cannot grasp. To put it more pragmatically, there may not be an answer that the mind can be completely happy with.

VE: At the same time, we can learn more astronomy and get a broad view of our solar system and galactic relationships. I'm often told that this is the great mystery, that the human mind probably cannot comprehend the vastness of creation at this moment in evolution. Nonetheless, aside from some new scientific information I do intuitively have a heartfelt sense about life's grandeur and magnificence, and I may have to be satisfied with that.

IF: You took the words out of my mouth. Although I said there's no answer that the human mind can be happy with, the heart can be satisfied. The heart can be satisfied in many ways, including the richness of meditation. When the mind is very quiet one realizes that the greatest wisdom actually lies not in the mind at all, but in the heart. In the deepest part of our hearts we have an understanding about these matters which really can't be put into words. Perhaps the closest we can come to talking about that deep understanding is to talk about love.

Love is an incredible force in the universe that exists at many levels. It's not just an emotion. D.K., among others, uses the term Love/Wisdom, which joins two concepts we normally think of as separate. Of course, from a higher perspective they're not really separate. Divine love is a form of knowingness that brings a sense of fulfillment in which all of one's questions have been answered. When one is in that heartfelt state one does not even need to ask, "Who am I?" and "Where did I come from?" anymore than an infant who is totally enveloped in his mother's love needs to ask these questions.

VE: So while these energy blessings from the stars may make some sense to the mind that we possess at the present time, ultimately our connection with creation will continue to be that pervasive, heartfelt feeling of divine love and compassion which all great religions and spiritual teachers have proclaimed and promised.

☆ ☆ ☆ ☆ ☆ ☆ ☆ ☆ ☆ ☆ ☆ ☆ ☆ ☆ ☆☆ ☆ ☆ ☆ ☆ ☆ ☆ ☆

Please remember to allow one week between this and the next initiation.

Chapter II

SIRIUS – THE BLESSING OF AMPLIFIED & GLORIFIED CHRIST CONSCIOUSNESS

Commentary by Irving

Before receiving this or any of the other star initiations, it is necessary to receive the *Subtle Body Fortification Attunement* and *Anti-Glamour Initiation* as explained on pages 69-74. Like the other star initiations, you can receive this Sirian initiation by simply asking for it (after doing the *Subtle Body Fortification Attunement* and *Anti-Glamour Initiation*). It is recommended that you **read this chapter** before asking for and receiving this initiation. Like the other star initiations, it takes about an hour and a quarter to receive the entire initiation. Please refer to page 79 to review the star initiation process.

The purpose of this Sirian initiation is to facilitate humanity's development of universal love—love of God, love of neighbor, love of the Earth and her creatures, and indeed…love for all of God's creation. In Western cultures this state of universal love has been called Christ Consciousness. However, it is vital to understand that this state should not only be associated with Christianity. Even so, the heart of Christ Consciousness can be expressed and understood by considering the following passage from the gospel according to Matthew 22:34-40.

> When the Pharisees heard that Jesus had silenced the Saducees, they gathered together, and one of them, a lawyer, asked him a question to test him.

"Teacher, which commandment in the law is the greatest?" Jesus said to him, "'You shall love the Lord your God with all your heart, and with all your soul, and with all your mind.' This is the greatest and first commandment. And a second is like it: 'You shall love your neighbor as yourself.' On these two commandments hang all the law and the prophets."

However, there is much more to Christ Consciousness than love. This universal level of consciousness also requires a profound grounding. In general, when I talk about grounding, I mean the movement of energy from a less dense plane to a more dense plane. Grounding implies willingness and dedication to implement this love, for we are not talking about just an abstract sentiment like "Oh, I just love everybody so much"—but a true love that demands daily expression and even sacrifice. By grounding we also include connection to Mother Earth. Notice how often Jesus explains his teachings through agricultural metaphors. He speaks of seeds, fruit, vines, the harvest, and such. This is the language of someone deeply connected to and deeply in love with Earth. Many of the energies in the New Age movement that are labeled as Christ energies lack that element of grounding. They are actually used as a way of escaping from daily life rather than helping us in the hard work of implementing our love in practical ways. To expand further on what is involved in achieving the mastery of Christ Consciousness, we need to understand how this state is related to the Seven Rays of Creation. These seven rays are the fundamental energy "building blocks" out of which everything—including Christ Consciousness—manifests. Each of the seven rays has innumerable lessons to teach humanity. These include the seven aspects of Christ Consciousness listed below, with the first aspect relating to the First Ray, the second aspect relating to the Second Ray, etc. (See **Appendix A** for a brief description of the seven rays themselves.)

The Seven Aspects of Christ Consciousness

1. Complete synthesis of personal and divine will.

2. Unconditional love for all of God's creation.

3. A profound union of being and action, so that one's life becomes an integrated set of actions implementing the Divine plan in the physical world.

4. Harmonization—a primary aspect of Christ Consciousness often achieved through conflict. This includes both internal harmonization of the many aspects of one's own being—and external harmonization between individuals and between different parts of society.

5. "Divine shrewdness"—a grounded, practical understanding for implementing God's plan.

6. Total devotion to God and to the belief that God's kingdom can fully manifest itself here on Earth.

7. A profound integration of spirit and matter within oneself and a profound comprehension of the relationship between spirit and matter. This includes the following understandings:

> a) That attachment to matter and to the physical senses is a major stumbling block to spiritual growth—with the attachment to wealth being a particularly insidious problem.
> b) That matter and spirit are a duality does not imply an intrinsic conflict between them. Matter is seen as the outer garment of God.
> c) That we are only fulfilled as human beings when we have unified matter and spirit, because it is our destiny to live in two worlds at once.

While this Sirian initiation works with all seven primary aspects of Christ Consciousness, it particularly focuses on aspect number two—*unconditional love for all of God's creation.* In terms of the chakra system it focuses mainly on opening and grounding the heart chakra. In our pursuit of being able to give and receive love, all of us have been emotionally wounded, either in childhood or in our adult life. Therefore, for the heart chakra to come more fully open, these wounds must be addressed and healed, to one degree or another. Even though it is not a primary purpose of this initiation to resolve these wounds directly since the energies mostly foster a sense of nurturing and belonging—it is possible that as the energies start their work you may feel a sense of tenderness or woundedness in the heart chakra. If this occurs, it typically lasts no more than two to three days at the most.

This initiation relating to Christ Consciousness comes to you from masters associated with the star Sirius, the brightest star in the night sky. Its preeminence is caused, not so much by its inherent brightness (about 23 times brighter than our Sun), but rather to its closeness to Earth. Located about 8.6 light-years away, Sirius is one of Earth's nearest neighbors.

The name Sirius comes from the Greek word *seirios* meaning sparkling or scorching. The Greeks also had other names for Sirius. Sometimes they referred to it simply as Astron, which is also the root from which our word astronomy derives. Sirius was also known as the Dog Star because of its prominence in the constellation Canis Majoris (the Greater Dog), where Sirius is positioned as the nose of the dog. Other cultures, including the Babylonians and some of the North American Indians, also saw the outline of a dog in this group of stars.

To find Sirius in the night sky—in the Northern hemisphere—first locate the constellation Orion and the three stars which make up Orion's belt. Orion's belt points almost directly to Sirius, which is down and to the left. When it is near the horizon, Sirius is a particularly beautiful star to observe, often appearing to change color—white, blue, green, orange, etc. This phenomenon is due to scintillation and is not a property of the star itself. It is the result of the distortion of the star's light as it passes through the atmosphere. The lower and brighter a star, the more prominent its scintillation. In addition to being the brightest star in the Earth's night sky, because Sirius is closer to the horizon, its light travels through more atmosphere than stars located directly overhead.

In 1862 it was discovered that Sirius is actually a binary star system with a companion star, Sirius B, which is ten thousand times dimmer than the bright primary star, Sirius A. Sirius B was the first "white dwarf" star to be discovered. White dwarves are the remains of old stars which have used up most of their fuel and collapsed. These collapsed remnants are so dense that a tablespoon full of Sirius B's matter would weigh about 2.5 tons.

Since ancient times Sirius has been known and revered in all the world's cultures. In ancient Atlantis the central mysteries were based on information received from masters associated with Sirius. Indeed, a fact not commonly known is that the name for Atlantis, in the language that the ancient Atlanteans spoke, means "The Home of Sirius." With the sinking of Atlantis, knowledge of the Sirian mysteries spread to Egypt where the star was associated with Isis. As early as 3000 B.C. the Egyptians celebrated the heliacal rising of Sirius (its dawn appearance after it had been missing from the sky for—depending on the observer's latitude—approximately two months) by declaring that day to be the first day of the new year. Shortly after the reappearance of Sirius, the Nile River would have its annual life-giving flood.

It is very appropriate that the initiation for Christ Consciousness should come from the masters of Sirius. These great masters have long been working with many different cultures on Earth to facilitate the development of Christ Consciousness, though that consciousness has been known by innumerable names at different times and places. Indeed, Sirius is the home of Christ Consciousness not only for our planet and solar system but for other portions of the galaxy. Christ Consciousness is the soul's unconditional love descended and expressed in living matter. For more information on the relationship between Sirius and the Christ see The Rays and the Initiations by Alice Bailey, p. 415.

According to D.K., it would be difficult to overestimate

the importance of the Sirian influence for planet Earth because Sirius is "that stupendous Source of our entire planetary life" discussed in The Rays and the Initiations, p. 687. The Sirian Spiritual Hierarchy has from the earliest times been the spiritual prototype for, and played a vital role in, the evolution of planet Earth's own Spiritual Hierarchy and therefore of humanity. Just as humanity is inspired and guided by our Spiritual Hierarchy, so the Sirians are inspired and guided by the Sirian masters.

Referring to Earth's Spiritual Hierarchy with the synonym "The Great White Lodge," D.K. reveals in The Rays and the Initiations, p. 415, that the entire work of the Great White Lodge is controlled from Sirius. He explains how spiritual energy streams forth from Sirius into the heart chakra of our Sun (which he calls the "Heart of the Sun") and from there to our own Spiritual Hierarchy. From Earth's Spiritual Hierarchy it then streams to individual initiates and disciples, and from there to humanity at large.

The importance of the Sirian masters is more profound than just guiding Earth's spiritual masters and humanity. As D.K. teaches us in Esoteric Astrology, p. 355, it was in part shepherding by the Sirian Lodge that fulfilled the Divine plan, which transformed animal man into ensouled man. Along with other talents, the Sirians are expert at helping souls anchor into matter. The soul's capacity to anchor spirit into physical worlds is the foundation of our growth, evolution, and eventual mastery.

There is a long road of spiritual development one must travel to become a master in Earth's Spiritual Hierarchy. Indeed, becoming such a master involves concurrent advancement along three paths of initiation sequences: planetary, solar, and Sirian. It is often said that a master is one who has taken the fifth solar initiation, but this is a simplification. In Initiation Human and Solar, p. 18, D.K. tells us that a master is one who has taken the seventh planetary initiation, the fifth solar initiation, and the first Sirian or cosmic initiation. As you might infer from the fact that becoming a master on Earth makes one only a beginning level Sirian initiate, the Sirius initiations are clearly the most advanced of the three levels.

As we mentioned before, Sirius played a primary role in the religious and cultural life of the ancient Egyptians, and the ancient Egyptian initiates worked intimately with masters from Sirius. Through the energy technologies received from these masters *the ancient Egyptians became expert at bringing in the etheric level of the soul.* The frequencies they used also developed many supernormal powers such as the ability to control thought forms in oneself and others. Unfortunately, despite the admonitions of their teachers, *some* of the ancient Egyptians seriously abused these powers. Because of the potential for abuse contained within these energy technologies, the Earth's Spiritual Hierarchy did not allow these initiations to be reinstituted after the ancient mysteries schools died out. Consequently, these frequencies have been missing from our subtle body fields down into modern times. Many people feel this lack unconsciously, though they do not know consciously what this feeling means. Permission was granted to one of the co-authors of this book (Irving Feurst) to restore these frequencies in a recreated Egyptian mystery school, provided that certain specific conditions were met to prevent abuse of supernormal powers.

Besides working with individuals to facilitate the development of Christ Consciousness, the Sirian masters also apply their talents to helping the Earth's gridwork system both directly and indirectly. They do this directly by adding certain frequencies to the gridwork system. They do it indirectly by utilizing frequencies which prepare for the activation of the *Sirian template* within each person. Each person who has incarnated on the Earth has a Sirian template, or gridwork pattern of energy, which is intended to greatly accelerate the development of Christ Consciousness. The template will not be activated all at once but in twelve distinct, though interrelated, stages. No activation of the template can occur until the water in our cells has been sufficiently structured so that it can hold more energy and information. The general need for structured water in our cells is a primary reason why both the Betelgeuse and Rigel masters are dedicated to assisting humanity at this time and in the future.

Activation of the Sirian template also facilitates activation of the seven Christ Seeds, and the activation of these seeds in turn facilitates further the activation of higher stages of the Sirian template. Recall that these Christ Seeds were mentioned in the Arcturian chapter. Each seed is associated with one of the seven rays and helps to develop one of the primary attributes of Christ Consciousness, described earlier in this chapter. Once the second Christ Seed becomes active, it significantly increases the capacity of the water in our cells to hold Second Ray energy. We will then be able to benefit from energies which the Sirian masters will send us to speed up the activation of the higher stages of the template. The Christ Seeds, the water in our cells, and energies from Sirius are interconnected in many ways. It isn't necessary to understand these transformative connections to benefit from them!

Just as with frequencies used in the ancient Egyptian mysteries, certain frequencies in the present Sirian template can lead to the development of supernormal powers. For this reason it can only be activated in a person who has achieved a large degree of freedom from glamour or when there is other assurance given to the Spiritual Hierarchy that these powers will not be abused. Also, for humanity as a whole, the template will be activated only when we are closer in time to the appearance of the World Teacher. Readers of this book should be wary of those who say that they will activate this energy template for them. The time is not yet ripe.

Conversation between Irving and Virginia

VE: This information about Sirius contains many challenging concepts such as how the Sirians could help ensoul "animal man." Why are the Sirians relating to our souls in the first place when it's God who created human souls?

IF: That's a very good question, Virginia. The soul itself does come directly from God. However, what we have to remember is that we are a soul in physical incarnation, and the process of a soul's incarnating into denser vibration involves a number of spiritual beings cooperating to accomplish the soul's mission. These helpmates include the person's Solar Angel (which some people refer to as the guardian angel) and the primary guides and teachers who assist that person. It also includes those spiritual beings who are entrusted with the overall guidance and evolution of humanity and planet Earth—such as the Sirians. You see, at a divine level we're all part of the same living mandala, and the separations that we make here on the physical plane do not really exist in higher planes.

VE: You've clarified that the Sirians, the Solar Angels, and guides are helpers on the soul's journey. But why does the soul need so many helpers to incarnate into matter at all?

IF: To understand the answer to this question we need to look at one of the great truths from the ancient mystery schools, a truth which helps us greatly in organizing our understanding of the universe. This truth is that there are two arcs of creation—the involutionary arc and the evolutionary arc. The involutionary arc is the descent of spirit into matter and has been called God's out-breath. The evolutionary arc is the ascent of matter into spirit and has been called God's in-breath. The personality is on the <u>ev</u>olutionary arc while the soul is on the <u>in</u>volutionary arc. Just as it is in the very nature of the personality to need help in expanding its consciousness and breaking exclusive identification with the ego, it is in the very nature of the soul to require help in descending and grounding into the realm of matter. For the most part our culture has lost touch with understanding the nature of the soul. People talk about the soul making wrong choices or losing its way. The soul is in profound union with God and is totally pure. The soul has no moral lessons to learn; rather the lessons of the soul have to do with learning how to descend into, and express itself through matter.

The descent of the soul into the vibration of matter does not happen all at once, but occurs in stages. To see why this is, we need to understand another great truth from the ancient wisdom. Indeed, this is probably the single greatest truth which the ancient wisdom has to teach us. It is the concept of "emanationism," meaning that God did not create the universe all at once, but rather through a series of emanations or planes of reality, each with different vibrational rates. In the Theosophical tradition the names given to these planes, which are seven in number, are the physical or etheric plane, emotional, mental, Buddhic, atmic, monadic, and cosmic or logoic. The soul issues forth from the monad, and therefore, there are five planes of reality below the soul. This explains the classic teaching found in Kabbalah, that the soul has five levels. As the soul descends through the planes of reality, the last plane into which it descends—namely the physical—has the densest vibration and is the most unfamiliar realm for the soul.

Those souls choosing to incarnate as humans on planet Earth are helped by the masters from Sirius in making this final step in their journey. The Sirians have been of inestimable help to humanity; they are experts at facilitating the descent of the soul into matter. This is why they were present to facilitate the transition of "animal man" into ensouled man, and it is also one of the main reasons why they are continuing to help us today.

The existence of the Sirian template is a continuation of this help because a main function of this template is to help anchor soul energy. This anchoring process helps both the individuals and the planet. It helps each individual anchor soul energy into the cellular level, and by the simultaneous presence of many individuals on the planet with their Sirian template activated, helps to anchor Christ energy into the planetary gridwork.

VE: All right, that clarifies the soul question. Now let's discuss this template to which you refer.

IF: It's an energetic gridwork structure which is present for all human beings who come into incarnation in the Earth. This gridwork's purpose, once it becomes activated, is to accelerate the development of all seven primary components of

Christ Consciousness. This template should not be confused with other energy structures readers may have heard about, such as the merkabah, etc.

VE: So where is that Sirian template located? In the subtle bodies, inside the physical body, or both?

IF: The template is located in both the physical and the subtle bodies, because one of the seven primary components of Christ Consciousness, harmonization, involves unification of the physical and the subtle bodies. Although the template works with the seven primary attributes of Christ Consciousness discussed earlier, its primary function is to anchor the spiritual realm into the physical realm, down to the cellular level. You see it's very important to realize that in order for Christ Consciousness to become fully manifest, we must physically change even down to the cellular level.

The increased structuring of water, which the two Orion initiations from Betelgeuse and Rigel help to bring about, also facilitates cellular level evolution. However, you will benefit the most from the cellular level help that non-terrestrial masters offer if you have first done considerable clearing work on your chakras, meridians, and subtle bodies.

VE: Then it is primarily a Sirian enterprise to help us get into this higher state of consciousness which the grid or the template represents?

IF: Yes, indeed. That's why I refer to it as a Sirian template because it utilizes Sirian energies, and its placement is under the guidance of the Sirian Spiritual Hierarchy. Even so, it's important to understand that the Sirians work in cooperation with masters from many other star systems. They're all part of a group mind. Their consciousness is all fused in a way that is almost impossible for a human being in a physical body to grasp. We can't really understand how it's possible for beings of this level to fuse their consciousness and yet at the same time maintain their individuality.

VE: All right, let's follow this to the conclusion. Someday there's going to be an evolutionary shift. At that point are the people of Earth, as we know ourselves today, somehow going to become Sirian?

IF: We will always be Earth beings. However, it's really an artificial distinction to draw a line and say here's the Earth influence and here's the Sirian influence. The two are inextricably intertwined. What will actually happen is that preceding the appearance of the World Teacher, there will be a series of incoming waves of spiritual energy that have been called "logoic" waves. (The logoic principle enables the Godhead to incarnate into matter and is the ultimate source of our inner divinity.) These waves will engulf the planet and will emanate jointly from our own Planetary Hierarchy and many of the non-terrestrial Spiritual Hierarchies who work in conjunction with Earth's spiritual mentors. After a certain number of these waves have passed through the Earth, then the Solar Angel or guardian angel of each individual will work in conjunction with the Sirian Spiritual Hierarchy to activate the first stage of the Sirian template. All of this together is to prepare humanity for the arrival of the World Teacher. When the World Teacher appears, the logoic waves and the first stage of the template will help people benefit from his or her teaching and ground the energies which emanate from the World Teacher. These energies will have the capacity to spark evolutionary shifts in humanity on all levels—physical, emotional, mental and spiritual.

The World Teacher will help people unify the energies of different spiritual traditions, and this unification will facilitate a new state of consciousness which we could call "superconsciousness." This state will unify different advanced states of consciousness from different traditions. The picture that I've been given is that the world's traditions fall into, from an energetic perspective, five major groupings corresponding to the elements. And when you do the advanced practices of a tradition that is in, say, the fire element family, there is a certain elixir that is secreted. Similarly, an elixir is produced for each of the other elemental families. When I say elixir I'm really talking about a subtle energy that has a liquid feeling to it. Humanity is evolving to a superconsciousness, which is facilitated by the simultaneous presence of the five elemental elixirs. One of the functions of the World Teacher will be to accelerate people's ability to produce all five elixirs and thus accelerate the reaching of this new state of superconsciousness.

VE: So what do you say to the people who believe that we're in a free-will situation, that we're supposed to become masters by our own efforts and we don't need the Sirians or any external teacher?

IF: Well, there are really two ways that people have of looking at Christ Consciousness and how we're going to attain it. Some people say that since Christ Consciousness is latent in all of us, we can access it all by ourselves without any help. Other people emphasize accepting the help provided by the Spiritual Hierarchies and the World Teacher. The reality is that both of these things are true. Christ Consciousness is our birthright, and we can also benefit from the guidance and initiations of someone else in helping us to realize that state. Those people who want to de-emphasize the role of the World Teacher are often coming from a very noble place in that they understand at a deep level that everyone is equal before God. However, common sense tells us we can learn from those wise ones who have been around far longer than we have. Of course, these masters do not consider themselves superior to anyone else. In the introduction of the Alice Bailey books when D.K. is describing who he is, he doesn't even use the word master to describe himself. He uses the word disciple. He goes on to say, "I am a brother of yours, who has traveled a little longer upon the Path than has the average student, and has therefore incurred greater responsibilities." That's really the bottom line.

VE: Coming back to the Sirian initiation, how does their expression of love relate to our previous Pleiadean initiation, which also involved love?

IF: Universal love is a constant, but the energies that manifest it differ from each other. For example, within the spectrum of the Pleiadean energies the yin aspect dominates, whereas within the Sirian energy spectrum the yang dominates. However, the Sirian energy also has a potent yin aspect—and needs the balance of both to be complete. Similarly, the energies from all seven of the initiations complement each other like the colors of the rainbow. I believe it's a mistake to rely on only one non-terrestrial energy to help your spiritual development.

Of the Seven Rays of Creation, the one that is most strongly represented within the Sirian energy spectrum is an assertive form of the Second Ray, the Ray of Love/Wisdom. The association of Sirius with the Second Ray is well-known. However, what is not so often appreciated is that Sirius is emitting all seven of the rays. The next most strongly represented ray is the First Ray, the Ray of Will and Power. Certain of the Sirian First Ray frequencies have a pronounced cyclical variation. A star's output of subtle energies, such as the seven rays, goes through cycles just as its output of physical energy does. Closer to Earth we experience that variations in physical energy can cause unwanted effects. For example, a variation in sunspots can affect electromagnetic communications as well as our health. Similarly, variations in subtle energy, both in our solar system and beyond, can also affect our lives here on Earth. When these Sirian subtle energy frequencies of will and power peak and travel to the Earth, their presence can be problematic because they can bring up people's unresolved issues around will, power, control, dominance and anger. Some people recognize that these issues are coming up from within themselves, but others assume the cause is outside of themselves and display intolerance or even violent behavior. *I emphasize that there is nothing intrinsically "bad" about these frequencies; the difficulty is that some people are not evolved enough to handle them.* These frequencies are part of the cyclical variations of nature and like physical cycles are beyond human control.

Some students of Sirian energy have suspected that a peak of these First Ray frequencies may have been a contributing factor to the timing of the Second World War. My own guidance confirms this information is correct. In any event, what is relevant for us currently is that there will be another peak of these First Ray energies around the year 2015. That is one reason why the Spiritual Hierarchy has been intensifying its efforts in recent times to accelerate humanity's spiritual evolution—so much so that many people who are sensitive to energy, feel that they are being pushed as fast as they can go. The goal is to minimize the unwanted effects of these First Ray frequencies by raising the consciousness of as many people as possible by 2015, so they can be an active force for love. Fortunately, some very positive changes will occur by 2012, as will be explained in Chapter 12. In the meantime humanity will be receiving support in many forms, including the initiations in this book.

VE: Granted that there are awesome cosmic energies affecting our planet all the time, I hope we aren't using those cyclical influences to avoid our own personal responsibilities for growth and healing.

IF: I agree. Furthermore, we can even use the effects of such things as the Sirian First Ray of Will and Power energy peaks to our advantage by working on our unresolved issues. It is reassuring to know that the spiritual realm always responds to our requests for help, both individually and collectively.

It is imperative to remain hopeful about the long-term response of humanity to the Sirian First Ray energy peaks! Eventually we will achieve the state of consciousness exemplified by the Sirians who are so advanced that as D.K. says, in the Alice Bailey writings, "Evil as we know it does not even exist on Sirius."

VE: That brings me to a question about evil. Why is it that beings of negative consciousness, with unloving intentions and actions, are allowed on this planet? How can we ever have the peace that we're supposed to implement as long as we're surrounded, and sometimes apparently outnumbered, by people who either are unconscious or are deliberately cruel, mean, violent and so forth?

IF: Well that's a very wonderful question. It's a profound question, and it's, of course, a question that people have been asking for centuries. I guess there are three things I want to say about that. The first one has to do with, "What is evil?" The second point has to do with, "Why does God allow evil?" And the third point is, "What can we do about it?" As I said in the Betelgeuse chapter, evil is good that hasn't arrived, because from an ultimate perspective there's only God. Darkness is simply an absence of light, and this is also what evil is. Evil is an absence of light. *Evil is good that is distorted.*

So why does God allow evil? The greatest gift that God has given all of us is the gift of free will. This is the natural birthright of all sentient beings, and it's important to realize this. It's important to realize how fundamental free will is to the structure of the universe. We don't have free will as human beings because we have decided, either consciously or unconsciously, to have free will. We have free will because God gave that as a gift to all sentient beings. So ultimately, what we're learning is how to manifest divine love in the physical world.

VE: That's why I always say, "Choice requires contrast."

IF: That's a good point. What I was about to say was that what sense would it make if the person you loved the most deeply and whose love makes you feel good inside came up to you and said, "I-love-you-very-much" in a very robotic way. What meaning would that have to you? It is also true, as you say, that in the phenomenal world good does not exist without what we call evil. Even God cannot create universes arbitrarily. Even God creates subject to certain restrictions; restrictions are built into logic, you might say. Even God can't create a universe in which there is only up and no down. The very concept of up implies that there is a down. So God has given all beings free will. Now it's up to us what we're going to make of that. Evil exists because there are individuals who have abused free will.

What do we do when we're confronted with evil? There are different levels at which one can respond to negativity, and in a given situation we may have to choose between them.

However, the highest level is one in which we oppose evil not by violence, but by shining forth the truth of God's love all the more.

VE: Which is what Jesus meant by saying, "Turn the other cheek."

IF: Yes. Exactly. We do live in the physical realm, and sometimes we find that we're in situations where we deviate from this highest principle. The point is to always realize that when you behave in a violent way, you are deviating from the higher principle. And we must also realize that when we engage in violence we incur the risk of becoming evil ourselves. There's a tendency for us to become like whatever we fight.

VE: Now, returning to the seven Christ Consciousness aspects which you listed as being requirements of spiritual masters, I have to say when I was reading those seven items I felt really quite overwhelmed. And I don't think I'll be alone in feeling that way when others also read those seven topics...Complete synthesis of personal and divine will...Unconditional love for all of God's creation...and so on. What can you say to cheer a person who's sincere but isn't sure how to incorporate those Seven Rays of Creation and acquire these seven vital aspects of Christ Consciousness?

IF: There are two things I'd like to say about that. The first and most important point is that we should have patience with ourselves. It can indeed seem overwhelming when we compare our spiritual level to the level which Jesus or any of the masters have attained. It can really make us feel very insignificant. However, it's important to realize that spiritual evolution is a lengthy process, not a one-act play. We need to have the attribute of *divine patience*. It's also important to understand there are psychological reasons why many people who are spiritually-oriented push themselves. This usually comes from issues originating in their family of origin and the need for approval from them. God totally approves of us and loves us just as we are. We have only to look at the teachings of Jesus himself to see how often he emphasized this—especially in the parable of the prodigal son. Until we become more self-accepting we will always be dissatisfied with our progress and lose the joy of the present moment.

The second idea I want to emphasize is that the most important tools for speeding up our spiritual growth are meditation and energy work, in that order, as I have previously mentioned.

VE: In order for our souls to be incarnated through a personality that expresses clarity and joy, we need to appreciate and utilize the many gifts of consciousness and energy already around us. Things like the various religions, and our esoteric teachings...remembrance of the great masters who came to teach us...the beauty of the wondrous planet and her many unique life forms...our loving brothers and sisters.

What are the Sirians presently offering to help us express this physical incarnation in a more joyous and growing way?

IF: The primary gift the Sirians bring us is the knowledge of universal love (Christ Consciousness) and guidance about how to develop it. They do this not only through the teachings they have communicated through D.K. and others, but through the energies they infuse into the human family and Mother Earth's gridwork systems. Although not everyone is conscious of energies from Sirius and other nonterrestrial sources, they are nonetheless manifesting in society's attitudes and actions. These guiding energies have fostered the ecology movement, feminism, holistic health, positive scientific inventions, and awareness of non-physical reality, among other changes.

An example of a very helpful and potent Sirian energy is the one you can receive through requesting the Christ Consciousness initiation described in this chapter. This initiation is allied to the two preparatory initiations and six preceding star initiations.

VE: It's my belief that the spiritual masters from Sirius have been humanity's mentors for eons of time and have repeatedly aided and guided us through the ups and downs of evolution's challenges. They have been loyal and constant in helping us awaken to our inner beauty, wisdom and love—and in assisting our efforts to attain higher consciousness for the benefit of all life.

We may be assured that the Sirians and other star masters who have also served humanity's progress will continue to offer their teachings, support and energies through the exciting times yet to be revealed. Truly we can await the Divine plan's unfoldment with joyful anticipation, knowing we are surrounded by our spiritual mentors and their eternal caring.

Even as children are safe in their parents' embrace, we too can have the spiritual nurturing that was promised long ago in the biblical statement: "I will not leave you comfortless."

☆ ☆ ☆ ☆ ☆ ☆ ☆ ☆ ☆ ☆ ☆ ☆ ☆ ☆ ☆ ☆☆ ☆ ☆ ☆ ☆ ☆ ☆ ☆

This is the seventh and final initiation. If you have received the initiations in an order other than given in this book, please remember to allow one week between this and the next initiation.

Chapter 12

NEW HOPE FOR HUMANITY

Commentary by Irving

Throughout this book Virginia and I have talked about how many spiritual masters—both those from our own Spiritual Hierarchy as well as non-terrestrial masters—are sending energy to facilitate the evolution of the Earth and of humanity. So where is all this headed? What is the future of planet Earth and of humanity? It will help us better understand the answers to these questions if we step back and look at the overall design of the universe and see how planetary and human evolution fit into that bigger picture.

As we discussed previously, the universe is composed of two arcs of creation—the involutionary arc and the evolutionary arc. The involutionary arc is associated with the descent of spirit into matter and has been called the out-breath of God. The evolutionary arc is associated with the ascent of matter into spirit and has been called the in-breath of God. The ultimate purpose of all evolutionary processes within the universe is the integration of these two arcs, the integration of matter and spirit. At the individual level we are talking about the integration of our spiritual nature and our personality (with the personality referring to our bodies, emotions, and thoughts). Many of the problems that we humans experience are the result of different ways in which the lack of integration between our spiritual nature and our personality can manifest. Some people have an inner emptiness, often unrecognized consciously, because their personality cannot even accept the reality of the spiritual realm. Other spiritually-oriented people have great difficulty integrating their spiritual experiences and values into daily life. A number of them have difficulty even accepting their life on the physical plane and long to return to higher realms.

There is certainly meant to be a natural polarity or tension between matter and spirit. However, recall from our discussion in the Rigel chapter that matter and spirit are not just opposites, but a duality. They are, therefore, complementary opposites. The tension between matter and spirit is a creative one, one that has the capacity to nourish us. But because so many people feel primarily fragmented by this tension, it's natural to wonder whether humanity is not meant to be much further along in the process of integrating matter and spirit than it is. Can we point to specific historical events that somehow resulted in humanity's being spiritually detoured?

Indeed, there are two historical factors which together have significantly delayed humanity's progress in unifying matter and spirit. The first of these factors is Jesus' physical death before he was able to set up a systematic method for transmitting certain information and energy initiations from one generation to the next—gifts that he wished to bequeath to humanity. To appreciate the last statement, we need to understand the difference between the mainstream or exoteric Christian interpretation of Jesus and the esoteric interpretation of Jesus. In the mainstream Christian interpretation Jesus is uniquely the Son of God who came to be people's savior. In the esoteric interpretation, all of us are equally sons or daughters of God, and Jesus' mission, through his teachings and an esoteric system of initiation, was to facilitate people's ability to access the higher states of consciousness known in the West as Christ Consciousness (which we discussed in the Sirian chapter).

In one esoteric interpretation, Jesus' physical death was not part of a divine plan for human salvation because it could not have been foreseen with absolute certainty. Human beings have free will, and this includes the particular individuals responsible for Jesus' physical death. Certainly, if Jesus came to teach us that we are all equally children of God, then the mainstream Christian interpretation of God sacrificing an only son needs to change. In actuality, Jesus' physical death was premature and prevented him from establishing the shakti lineage that he intended. It is true, as some have claimed, that parts of Jesus' original esoteric teachings and initiations have survived; but they exist only in fragmented form, not as a whole and coherent system.

The energies that Jesus meant to bequeath were inspired variations of energies from the Jewish mystical tradition of Kabbalah, to which he was heir. In addition to being a spiritual genius, Jesus was also a Kabbalistic genius with deep and original insights into the energies used in his time. He saw, even though Kabbalistic energies were thought to be governed primarily by the metaphysical fire element, that the metaphysical water element had a much greater part in the operation of these energies than previously supposed. For example, the water component is responsible for the characteristic way that many Kabbalistic energies gradually integrate deeper and deeper into the body, much like physical water can sink slowly but deeply into the Earth. Following divine guidance, Jesus cooperated with a consortium of many non-terrestrial masters, including those from Rigel, Betelgeuse, and Sirius, to create a system of Kabbalistic initiation that emphasized fire and water equally.

In his public ministry Jesus tried to develop in people the quality that has been called "Divine Vision," the ability to see the world more in the way that God sees it. For example, those with Divine Vision see all people as equally the children of God and see the loving support of God throughout nature. The main way that Jesus taught was through parables, which are attempts to wake us up from the trance induced by worldly concerns and to see and feel the reality of God's unconditional love for us. Jesus' concern with developing Divine Vision also greatly influenced the Kabbalistic system of initiation that he helped to co-create. A key part of that initiatory system was a Kabbalistic shakti that developed both Divine Vision as well as the capacity to feel God's loving presence in one's body. Jesus called this energy "The Foundation," both because it was one of the foundations of the system and also because he believed Divine Vision should be the foundation from which all of our actions stem. This energy is one of the main gifts that he intended to bequeath to humanity; however, he died prematurely before he could set up a lineage for the transmission of either this energy or the rest of his system.

Following Jesus' physical death, the Earth's Spiritual Hierarchy and the cooperating non-terrestrial masters could not find anyone with the genius to understand his system or with the charisma to set up a lineage with worldwide influence. If masters want to send energy to help humanity they can do it in two ways: either through energies that are meant to be communicated to people directly in initiations or through energies that are sent to the Earth's gridwork and which thus reach people indirectly. Although the gridwork approach affects human spiritual evolution much more slowly, this was the only approach available to the masters for getting Jesus' energies to humanity following his physical death. These energies are vital if humanity is to fully develop Divine Vision, the integration of matter and spirit, and those states known in the West as Christ Consciousness.

We want to emphasize that there are many beautiful and spiritually transformative energies from many traditions that have been present throughout history and continue to be present today. *We are not saying that Jesus' energies are the only ones, nor are we saying that they are the most important ones.* Their primary significance at this point in time comes from the fact that they are missing; that they are not present in the Earth's gridwork system or in our subtle bodies to the degree they would be if Jesus' system had been passed on.

The fact that Jesus' energies were not passed on as a system of initiation is the first of the two historical factors referred to above. The second factor has to do with the history of a secret guild of spiritually developed humans called "Earth Keepers." Throughout history these Earth Keepers have existed in cultures all over the world and have had the responsibility of helping to maintain the welfare of the Earth's subtle energy gridwork system, as well as adding new energies to facilitate the spiritual evolution of humanity. The Earth Keepers put into the Earth's gridwork both energies received from previous generations of their guild as well as energies received from terrestrial and non-terrestrial masters.

One of the main reasons they have worked in secret is that the energies they use, like many advanced spiritual energies, can develop supernormal powers. The number of Earth Keepers at any given time has always been relatively small because each generation has difficulty in finding successors who are both talented enough and can also be trusted with the supernormal powers. However, even though their number is small, the presence of these Earth Keepers is critical because certain frequencies of energy can be placed into the gridwork only by physically-embodied beings.

Many advanced spiritual energies cannot be safely present in the Earth's gridwork system unless that system is sufficiently strong. One of the factors affecting the Spiritual Hierarchy's ability to continue sending Jesus' frequencies to the Earth's gridwork after his transition was the combined effort of the Earth Keepers in many lands. These Earth Keepers, with the help of the Office of the Christ, continuously strengthened the Earth's gridwork to hold higher and higher levels of Jesus' energies. Since Jesus' system consists of a graduated sequence of higher and higher frequencies, the vibration of the Earth's gridwork must be stepped up before each subsequent frequency level can be integrated.

A key event in the history of the Earth Keepers occurred after the Romans invaded Celtic Britain in 43 A.D. By the time the Romans eventually left in 410 A.D., they had effectively destroyed Celtic civilization as it had previously existed. Very sadly, only a few generations after the initial Roman invasion, the Celtic branch of the Earth Keepers no longer existed. Many were killed by the Romans, and the few who remained very reluctantly chose not to leave successors rather than pass their knowledge to those who could not be trusted with the development of supernormal powers.

Following the physical death of Jesus, even though his system was no longer available in human initiations, many terrestrial and non-terrestrial masters began the process of putting these key frequencies into the Earth's gridwork. Then gradually, over time, they began building up the levels of these needed frequencies. Following the demise of the Celtic Earth Keepers, the levels of Jesus' energies that were already in the gridwork system remained present, but the gridwork lacked additional ongoing frequency upgrades necessary for higher vibrational levels. Consequently, the cumulative effect of Jesus' premature transition and the demise of the Celtic Earth Keepers have significantly slowed the evolution of humanity's ability to integrate matter and spirit. Again, we are *not* saying that Jesus' energies are the only ones that can develop this ability; nor are we saying that they are the most important. The emphasis is on the fact that the higher levels of these energies are missing. *A key concept here is that the combined presence of energies from many different spiritual traditions, both in the Earth's gridwork and in our subtle bodies, is required before humanity can reach the highest stages of spiritual evolution.*

The story does not end here! The message of this chapter is really one of hope because events will soon take a much more positive turn. For many centuries the masters have had an ongoing project of finding ways to substitute for the missing frequencies of the Celtic Earth Keepers and of developing alternative paths for strengthening the gridwork's capacity to receive new and higher levels of Jesus' missing frequencies. *The good news is that this project will be completed in the year 2012 A.D.!* At that time there will also be one or more spiritual groups present who will be capable of restoring initiations with Jesus' original Foundation energy. The changes in the Earth's gridwork and the restoration of this particular part of Jesus' system will greatly accelerate humanity's spiritual evolution, including the critical capacity to integrate matter and spirit. It will also prepare the way for the appearance of the spiritual leader who has been called the World Teacher and the even greater transformations that he or she will bring.

As mentioned, many of the world's traditions are awaiting the predicted appearance of a major spiritual leader. Buddhists are waiting for Maitreya Buddha, Muslims are awaiting the Imam Mahdi, Jews are awaiting the Messiah, and Christians are awaiting the Christ. The truth is that all of these leaders are the same figure. This World Teacher will appear not just for the people of one particular faith, but will come for people of all faiths, as well as for those who have no spiritual beliefs. This great being will be a new spiritual teacher rather than a former spiritual teacher reappearing.

The World Teacher will coordinate the efforts of many people and masters to bring about a Golden Era of peace, justice, and harmony for humanity. Through an extraordinarily profound connection to the Earth's gridwork system, the World Teacher will act as a conduit for a great influx of energies to the Earth and humanity from many terrestrial and nonterrestrial masters. *The World Teacher will also institute a system of energy initiations that will unify the energies from all of the world's spiritual traditions.* He or she will also introduce those energies needed to inaugurate the next cycle of the Divine plan.

It's important to understand that the World Teacher will be a spiritual leader, not a political one, and will possess authority only to the extent that people voluntarily give it. It is also important to understand that the World Teacher will not be some sort of spiritual king, but more like the head of a committee. To use another analogy, the World Teacher will have a relationship to humanity and the Earth that is similar to the relationship of a person's crown chakra to their entire chakra system. The Golden Era of humanity cannot be brought about by one person no matter how powerful, but requires the coordinated efforts of all of us working together.

Conversation between Virginia and Irving

VE: I'm sure that many readers will feel that your explanation about Jesus' transition before he could establish a shakti lineage (something like those of various Eastern cultures and religions) detracts from the stature of Jesus. How could such a premature transition even happen to someone of Jesus' extraordinary power, love, and wisdom? How could such a transition be consistent with the will of God?

IF: As someone who has the utmost respect for Jesus, I've certainly had to consider for myself the questions you just raised. I believe the information in this chapter is completely consistent with having a special reverence for Jesus.

Let me answer your first question about how a premature transition could have even happened to someone of Jesus' extraordinary power, love, and wisdom. It is critical to understand that, as long as Jesus was present here on the earth in a physical body, his life was impacted by the free will decisions of others. God has given the inviolable attribute of free will to all human beings, including the particular individuals responsible for the arrest and crucifixion of Jesus.

Why were these individuals so opposed to Jesus in the first place? Great spiritual leaders have a way of antagonizing those who wish to place worldly concerns over the spiritual. For example, the Buddha and Mohammed each had more than one assassination attempt made on their lives. Quite aside from the fact that such leaders can threaten existing political power, D.K. tells us that the energy field of any master can be very disturbing to those who are not prepared to grow spiritually. The energy field of Jesus was especially powerful. For one thing he was continuously emitting energies of Divine Vision and these energies can be particularly disturbing, because as they open your vision they can cause you to question all of your values and all that you have done in a whole lifetime. I have seen this happen in initiations I have given to students for awakening Divine Vision. Of course, these initiations use vastly less powerful energies than the ones emitted by Jesus' aura every day.

The antagonism which Jesus aroused was so great and eventually became so organized that the only way he could have overcome it was by being responsible, either directly or indirectly, for the deaths of others. His moral code prevented him from doing this. Therefore, his physical death should not be seen as a defeat, but rather as a victory because he was willing for his physical body to perish rather than violate his deeply-held beliefs about nonviolence.

I believe Jesus' willingness to have his physical body perish was consistent with God's will. I do not believe that it was God's intention that Jesus die on the cross from the beginning. I believe it was God's original intention that people follow Jesus, not kill him. However, I believe the decision Jesus made to go to the cross, after he was arrested and imprisoned by the Romans, did represent God's will. It is useful to distinguish, as a number of theologians have, between God's *antecedent* will and God's *consequent* will. Antecedent will refers to God's original intention with respect to a given situation, whereas consequent will refers to God's intention after the situation has been altered by the free will actions of human beings.

I emphasize again that Jesus' death should not be seen as a defeat. We should see the opposition he aroused as a testament to his power and see his willingness to go to his death rather than desert his belief in nonviolence as a testament to the purity of his actions and belief.

I believe that for us today Jesus' life and teachings are of greater significance than the circumstances surrounding his death. If Jesus' teachings live in your heart, then he was victorious—regardless of how he died.

VE: In spite of certain difficulties experienced by Jesus, his ultimate gift to humanity was his model and the teachings that he disseminated, not only to his disciples but to the many followers who were later able to influence an extraordinary number of human beings.

IF: Yes. His life was also a victory because his teachings changed the course of history. He still serves as a great model for all of us. I only wish that more Christian denominations today reflected the original intent of his esoteric teachings including his desire to create a shakti lineage.

VE: What is the position of Christianity today in terms of aiding the appearance of the next World Teacher?

IF: Those of the many Christian denominations that pass on true spiritual teachings are helping to prepare for the appearance of the World Teacher, as are all genuine spiritual teachings of all faiths. However, modern mainstream Christianity is doing nothing at all *from an energetic perspective* to prepare for the coming of the World Teacher. As mentioned, one of the great tragedies in the history of Christianity is the loss of the systematic passing on of the esoteric teachings and energies of Jesus. Fortunately, these teachings and energies have not been completely lost. Fragments do survive in scattered locations of the globe even though they have been lost as a coherent system.

One of the important things to understand about any great spiritual leader is that such a leader always passes on both exoteric, or outer teachings, and esoteric, or inner teachings. Any teacher of any subject who is a good teacher will teach different people in different ways depending on their level of consciousness and willingness.

It's also important to understand that the purpose of the esoteric teachings is not to create some kind of an elite. Esoteric teachings are a natural outgrowth of this universal principle of good teaching as well as several other important facts. One is that some of the most important truths about the universe are difficult to believe when you first hear them, and if they are revealed prematurely, a person is likely to reject a truth that is very important for their development. The second point to understand about esoteric spiritual teachings, which distinguishes them from purely intellectual pursuits, is that advanced spiritual practices can lead to the development of various supernormal powers which a good spiritual teacher does not want to pass on indiscriminately.

Esoteric teachings exist in all great spiritual traditions, and even in the New Testament we see places where Jesus tells things to the disciples that he does not tell to the general public. So part of the tragedy of current Christianity is that in an admirable attempt to be democratic—this attempt coming from the recognition that all of us are equal before God—people have corrupted and disempowered the original Christian teachings by denying their esoteric component. But this need not be a permanent situation because the spiritual forces that are guiding humanity are hoping that the full esoteric teachings that Jesus meant to pass on can be brought back. Perhaps this book can be instrumental in inspiring people who want to reinstitute Jesus' esoteric teachings.

VE: Instrumental in explaining that energy initiations are part of the Christian tradition?

IF: Right, exactly.

VE: Can you say more about why our beautiful planet's gridwork is incomplete and has been weakened—to our disadvantage?

IF: The gridwork as it now exists is seriously incomplete because necessary frequencies are missing due to a series of interrelated historical calamities. One of these involves the demise of the Celtic Earth Keepers, as previously mentioned. The Celtic Earth Keepers also used chanting and toning to bring in divine, subtle sound frequencies. They knew how to utilize Stonehenge to spread those frequencies throughout the planet's gridwork system. There were also other frequencies missing due to misuses of powers in ancient Egypt, which caused the subsequent withdrawal of certain initiations by the Spiritual Hierarchy. A series of calamities also occurred that preceded Egypt, going back to ancient Lemuria and Atlantis. That's really where the problems with Earth's gridwork started. Subsequent events, from ancient Egypt to modern times, are like knocking over of a row of karmic dominoes set up in ancient Lemuria and Atlantis.

VE: So these damages to the gridwork affected human consciousness and their ability to use energies appropriately.

IF: Absolutely, and the missing frequencies in the Earth's gridwork system affect us all in our daily lives very profoundly, in ways that most people don't realize. Many people who are sensitive to energy have the feeling that there's something missing, that their energy body is not quite right, and that this lack goes deeper than the influences of their family of origin and of the society in which they now live. It's very important to understand that although our subtle bodies are made up of subtle matter, it is still matter and it must be renewed and replenished! In our physical body we know that cells divide and that we produce new cells as a result of the food that we eat. In a similar way, the subtle bodies have matter that is subject to the law of entropy and over time degrades and must be replaced. Where does this replenishment come from?

Let's take a look at the subtle mental body as an example. Most of the matter in our mental body is made from energy that we absorb from the Sun. The second most significant source of the matter in our mental body comes from trees, and there's a very profound connection between human mental bodies and the subtle energy field of trees. Many people sense this at an intuitive level. They know that when they are next to a tree their thinking is clearer and they feel more at peace. Because there are frequencies missing from the Earth's gridwork system, there are also very important frequencies missing from the energy fields of trees. Consequently, there are necessary frequencies missing from our mental bodies. Though most people aren't sensitive enough to energy to realize that something is missing, many people are, and that number is increasing.

VE: In nature, we go to the forest or the mountains, the oceans or the deserts, and we really feel physically invigorated. Sometimes that can be interpreted as a spiritual and an emotional uplift, too. And of course we must honor the physical body's oxygenation process!

IF: Yes. And it is certainly true that trees also have a profound effect on our emotional bodies. Indeed, there are these very intimate links that exist between the different kingdoms of nature—between the mineral kingdom, the animal kingdom, the plant kingdom, and the human kingdom—which must not be disrupted. People are becoming familiar with the concept of ecology on a physical level, and in a similar way realize you can't disrupt the subtle energy fields of any one kingdom without affecting all kingdoms.

VE: So our feelings that we're not as powerful as we should be, that we can't do all the things that we'd like to do, not only come from what you would call a psychological lack of worth and so on, but from a very deep inner sensory level of dissatisfaction. I hear many people saying how hard it is to be here on the planet knowing that they have something missing that can't quite be identified.

IF: Yes, many people have those feelings, and when they realize that there is some reason for them that can't be ascribed to just their family of origin, their society, or their environment—they often look for other reasons. These explanations might have to do with alien sources interfering with the Earth or something related to the DNA level. But the most important thing to emphasize is that the source of these feelings is not something exotic but is literally right under our feet. It's the very Earth—it's the water we drink and the air that we breathe—which lack certain energy frequencies. Indeed the reason these feelings can be so strong is because this lack surrounds us all the time in our daily life. We can't get away from the fact that everything we do is connected to Mother Earth.

These missing frequencies also influence people's spiritual development. Many people have had the experience of clearing themselves of certain negative thought forms only to have those return very quickly, leaving them at a loss to explain why is it so hard to remain clear of these unwanted thought forms. Of course, there are many reasons for this. However, one explanation is that our mental bodies are simply not as strong as they really should be at this point in time. If these missing frequencies were present in the Earth's gridwork, and therefore in the trees and in our mental bodies, it would be much easier for people to clear negative thought forms out of their mental bodies. Then more often we would all feel the way that we do mentally and emotionally when we're in a forest, in nature.

VE: The Cosmic Consortium and the Sirian coordinators of these seven energy blessing gifts to humanity and to the planet, which this book explains, come to help us achieve a greater sense of balance. It is heartwarming to know there is a divine plan underway to help each person and humanity as a group by linking us together in cooperative endeavors for a more joyful, more delightful experience of being in a body.

IF: Indeed, as the Earth's missing frequencies are filled-in, everyone will find it more joyful to be in a body. This will be particularly true for people who are consciously aware and sensitive to energy. There can be a real tendency for people to desire escaping from the body if they are sensitive to energy and notice the feeling that something is missing. However, the body is here for a reason, and we see that even when people evolve spiritually and become enlightened, they don't disappear in a puff of smoke or a flash of white light. They're still here in a body. *The real purpose of humanity's spiritual evolution is not transcendence but wholeness. We are not here to abandon the body but to unify body and spirit.*

As the missing frequencies get restored to the Earth's gridwork it will become easier for people to enjoy the experience of being in a body. Let us be grateful that many masters are working to help bring about this shift in the Earth's gridwork and have been working at this for centuries. These include the masters of our own Planetary Hierarchy and many non-terrestrial masters, including those discussed in this book. When the World Teacher does appear the whole process of restoring Earth's missing frequencies will be greatly accelerated, for this is one of the functions of the World Teacher. It cannot be over emphasized that the World Teacher will come to develop a spirituality that links people even more deeply to the Earth and that increases people's appreciation for Mother Earth and their own bodies.

VE: I hope that in the preceding eleven chapters we have emphasized the enormous contribution that a person who decides to accept these energy blessings from the stars is giving to themselves and all of life. And I wonder if there's something more you would like to say about the relationship between the Earth's gridwork system, human consciousness, and the World Teacher?

IF: Let me emphasize your point that through receiving these energy blessings from the stars every person has the opportunity to make an enormous contribution not only to their personal evolution but to the evolution of humanity and the planet. However, no one should feel obligated to ask for the energy blessings. It's also perfectly fine for someone to receive these initiations purely for the personal benefit that they will get from them. Nonetheless, because there is an intimate link between human beings and the Earth—as well as between all human beings—the changes that will take place in the person's energy field from receiving these initiations can have very far-reaching effects. The second point I would reiterate is that the presence of the coming World Teacher's energy field will intensify higher consciousness in many ways—in all of these links between individuals and in the links between an individual and the Earth's gridwork system. In brief, the World Teacher's energy will be like tying a string on a package. It's like completing the wrapping of a wonderful divine gift. This divine plan will usher in a Golden Era for humanity because of the actions that all of us will take collectively as we are inspired and uplifted by this great teacher and each other.

VE: So what is the relationship between the World Teacher and the level of vibration of the Earth's grid and the people on the planet being able to receive this being's energy?

IF: The Earth's gridwork system has to be developed in two ways in order for the appearance of the World Teacher to occur. The first is that it must be strong enough to hold both the very high vibrational energies which will be emitted by the energy field of the World Teacher and the very high vibrational energies which the World Teacher will communicate through initiation to other people who will then carry them. The second point is that the gridwork must not only be strong enough to carry these energies, but it must also be able to ground the energies into the physical Earth. Why? Because while these powerful energies will help humanity evolve, they're also coming to help *nature* evolve. These energies will actually shift the energy fields of many different plants and rocks, and those shifted fields will in turn affect the evolution of humanity. There are many intricate feedback loops here. So in order for the energy field of the Earth to be developed enough to ground the energies that will be emitted by the World Teacher, many subtle energy triangles have to be strengthened. As mentioned before, a particularly vital triangle is the one formed by the heart chakra of the Earth, the heart chakra of the Sun, and the heart chakra of Sirius. One of the critical functions of this essential triangle is to ground these energies that will be emitted by the World Teacher.

VE: Since we've talked so much about the changes that the World Teacher will bring, I need to suggest the possibility that the World Teacher could be a pair of beings or even a group of energies, not a single identity. And I should add that some people will undoubtedly disagree with the explanations concerning humanity's delayed spiritual progress. In any case I want to emphasize your previous point that the Golden Era of humanity cannot be brought in by the efforts of just one person, no matter how powerful. Rather, this new era must come from the efforts of all of us cooperating together with the sometimes inscrutable cosmic rhythms and cycles which affect our lives so profoundly and continuously guide our destiny. Since the effectiveness of that cooperation is dependent on each of us continuing to work on our own personal and spiritual evolution, it is my sincere hope that the energy blessings from the stars given in this book may help facilitate that evolution for those now willing to participate.

It's vital to understand that spirit is always mediated through a particular form, and for us that form is presently a human body. Let us answer the age old calling to serve our Creator by using the physical form at our disposal with wisdom, compassion, and love. These characteristics are our cosmic passport beyond time and space, yet they must be gained by our willingness to seek them within our inner consciousness where they await unveiling and expression.

IF: Yes. And with all of this talk about what the future will bring, let us not forget the many blessings with which we have been endowed and which we can enjoy in current time. Surely one of these blessings is the stars. Like the person on the cover of this book, let us go out into the night and raise our arms to the skies in celebration of their beauty and mystery. May we ever increase in knowledge and appreciation of their light and the light of the loving God who created them.

Appendix A

THE SEVEN RAYS OF CREATION

1. The ray of Will or Power. The prime cosmic function of the first ray is to initiate those actions necessary to the carrying out of the divine plan.

2. The ray of Love/Wisdom. The prime cosmic function of the second ray is to attract together those things necessary to the carrying out of the divine plan.

3. The ray of Intelligent, Creative Activity. The prime cosmic function of the third ray is to implement (oversee the details of) the divine plan.

4. The ray of Harmony and Harmony through Conflict. The prime cosmic function of the fourth ray is to bring about the harmonization of the polarities within creation.

5. The ray of Science and Concrete Knowledge. The prime cosmic function of the fifth ray is to use the mental plane to unify the lower and higher planes.

6. The ray of Devotion and Abstract Idealism. The prime cosmic function of the sixth ray is to turn hearts and minds to God.

7. The ray of Order and Mercurial change (Has also been described—we believe less well—as the ray of Ceremonial Order). "The prime cosmic function of the seventh ray is to perform the magical work of blending spirit and matter in order to produce the manifested form through which the life will reveal the glory of God." Esoteric Psychology, Volume One by Alice Bailey.

Appendix B

SOLAR ANGEL CONTRACT

I, _____,
(print name) hereby enter into the following contract with my Solar Angel. I do this freely, totally, irrevocably and without reservation.

I hereby give to my Solar Angel complete authority to determine the appropriateness of all energy work, work with devas, or work involving manifestation in which I am involved, directly or indirectly, as either sender or receiver. I give my Solar Angel "complete authority" to take whatever corrective actions it wishes whenever it decides any of the above three kinds of work is inappropriate.

Whenever in this contract I give my Solar Angel complete authority, I include giving it the right to make a decision that is final and need not involve any additional consultation on its part.

Whenever there is any question as to how to interpret any part of this contract, I give my Solar Angel complete authority to determine how that part should be interpreted.

I understand that this contract specifically includes giving my Solar Angel complete authority to modify or override the actions of my personal unconscious.

I understand that this contract represents a profound act of surrender to and trust in higher spiritual guidance.

Signature_____ Date_____

Appendix C

KEEPING AN INITIATION DIARY

We recommend that you keep a written record of your experiences while receiving the initiations in this book. For each separate initiation you request, first record the date, then the name of the initiation (such as Arcturus), and any experiences you noticed either during the initiation itself or in the days, weeks or months that follow. Articulating your experiences will help you to better understand and benefit from them. We often become quickly acclimated to improvements in our life, so referring back to your diary can remind you of how much you have changed. For people who are not that sensitive to subtle energy, the diary can help reinforce the reality of the transformations they have experienced.

We have reproduced below anonymous excerpts from five people's energy diaries to illustrate how people can have different reactions to the same initiation. All the excerpts are for the Arcturian initiation for hope.

"There is a wonderful calming feeling to this energy. The Arcturian energy is like dropping into a hot tub and having that relaxing feeling come through your body and soul."

"Certain major projects which had been halted through my lack of enthusiasm for them actually got underway…long term decisions were activated at this time. I have since moved and found myself the first full-time job in twenty years…twenty years of old paperwork have been thrown away and most of my old furniture dispatched to the auctioneers!"

"Feel slightly more optimistic in general."

"This initiation was very pleasant and I felt no effects afterward."

"I feel quite good, and yet there is a lot of difficult stuff going on around me. Feel a strong sense of connection, that I am on the right path towards home, and that I am safe and cocooned."

☆ ☆ ☆ ☆ ☆ ☆ ☆ ☆ ☆ ☆ ☆ ☆ ☆ ☆ ☆ ☆☆ ☆ ☆ ☆ ☆ ☆ ☆☆

Suggested Format for Your Diary

Keep a separate record for each initiation including date, name of initiation, and comments.

Date: _____ Initiation: _____

Comments: _____

_____

_____

_____

_____

_____

_____

_____

Date: _____ Initiation: _____

Comments: _____

_____

_____

_____

_____

_____

_____

_____

_____

☆ ☆ ☆ ☆ ☆ ☆ ☆ ☆ ☆ ☆ ☆ ☆ ☆ ☆ ☆ ☆ ☆☆ ☆ ☆ ☆ ☆ ☆ ☆ ☆

Date: _____ Initiation: _____

Comments: _____

_____

_____

_____

_____

_____

_____

_____

_____

ENERGY BLESSINGS *from the* STARS

Date: _____ Initiation: _____

Comments: _____

_____

_____

_____

_____

_____

_____

☆ ☆ ☆ ☆ ☆ ☆ ☆ ☆ ☆ ☆ ☆ ☆ ☆ ☆ ☆ ☆☆ ☆ ☆ ☆ ☆ ☆ ☆ ☆

Date: _____ Initiation: _____

Comments: _____

_____

_____

_____

_____

_____

_____

Date: _____ Initiation: _____

Comments: _____

_____

_____

_____

_____

_____

_____

_____

☆ ☆ ☆ ☆ ☆ ☆ ☆ ☆ ☆ ☆ ☆ ☆ ☆ ☆ ☆☆ ☆ ☆ ☆ ☆ ☆ ☆ ☆ ☆

Date: _____ Initiation: _____

Comments: _____

_____

_____

_____

_____

_____

_____

_____

ENERGY BLESSINGS from the STARS

Date: _____ Initiation: _____

Comments: _____

_____

_____

_____

_____

_____

_____

☆ ☆ ☆ ☆ ☆ ☆ ☆ ☆ ☆ ☆ ☆ ☆ ☆ ☆ ☆ ☆ ☆☆ ☆ ☆ ☆ ☆ ☆ ☆ ☆

Date: _____ Initiation: _____

Comments: _____

_____

_____

_____

_____

_____

_____

TRANSFORM YOUR CELLULAR WATER FIELD

Extraordinary audio tape recorded by Irving Feurst to accelerate your spiritual transformation!

Water. We cannot live without it, yet how many of us really understand its remarkable physical and spiritual properties—and the even more remarkable properties of water in living cells? As explained in the <u>Energy Blessings from the Stars</u> book, the water in your cells is not the same as tap water. Your cellular water is really a liquid crystal and, as such, is capable of holding information and subtle energy. As we evolve spiritually, the subtle energy field surrounding our cellular water becomes ever more organized, continually increasing its ability to hold information and hold higher vibrational energy.

Side one is an explanation and exploration of the mysteries of water. Side two is a remarkable guided meditation that releases a shakti—a metaphysical or spiritual energy that behaves intelligently—to accelerate the naturally occurring transformation of the energy field around your body's cellular water. The result is an acceleration of your spiritual evolution because your subtle bodies will be able to hold more information, more energy and higher vibrational energies.

This tape is imprinted with actual transformative frequencies that cannot be duplicated. Using this tape will increase the ability of your subtle bodies to benefit from shakti—the shaktis used in the initiations described in the <u>Energy Blessings from the Stars</u> book—as well as those used in many common forms of energy work. It is also possible that using this tape may deepen your meditations.

Single cassette tape T103 $12.95 60 minutes
Please use the order form on the next to last page.

 Spiritual Education Endeavors Publishing Company
1556 Halford Avenue #288, Santa Clara, CA 95051-2661 USA
(408) 245-5457

Did you know that the entire human race can be raised into a mass ascension experience? ...that photon energy could be used to raise our consciousness?... that alchemy may be closer than you think? What was the effect on our planet Earth of the comets' collision with Jupiter? Learn more about the true nature of time.

New Teachings for an Awakening Humanity, 1994/95 Revised Edition.

Here's an extraordinary book that has been highly recommended by Judith Skutch, A Course in Miracles; Eileen Caddy, Findhorn Community; and John Randolph Price, author. You will learn more about the true reason for Jesus' mission 2000 years ago and at the same time see a glimpse of the wondrous future that awaits us on Earth. "I come to advise you that humanity is not alone in the Universe...that your Earth is now being raised back into the higher love dimension she once held."— *The Christ*. The original text has been updated with over 50 pages of new information including two additional chapters titled the "Alchemy of Ascension" and "Your Natural Inheritance Reclaimed."

Virginia Essene, Editor

Spiritual Education Endeavors Publishing Company
1556 Halford Avenue #288, Santa Clara, CA 95051-2661 USA
(408) 245-5457

$9.95 paperback • 5.5 X 8.5 •264 pages • ISBN 0-937147-09-5
Library of Congress Catalog Card Number 94-068706

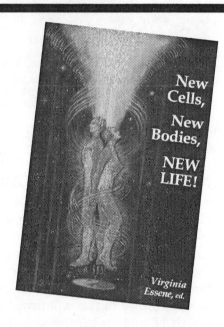

"Having trouble separating your delta waves from your thetas and super high Betas? Fear not: Tom Kenyon will help you get a grip on your consciousness, sub-consciousness, and altered consciousness in his book."

BRAIN STATES

TOM KENYON, M.A.

300 Pages • $11.95 Retail • ISBN 1-880698-04-9

Brain States, Kenyon, a psychologist and a musician, has spent years studying the effects of sound, music, and language on the human nervous system. Kenyon offers a technical excursion into how the brain works, noting the clear distinction between brain and mind. To do this he ascends to the heavens with Pegasus and drops by a shopping mall puddle to visit an amoeba. Through Kenyon's book, you will learn to overcome test anxiety, increase your intelligence, power your athletic abilities, hone your language skills, cure numerous psychological problems, tweak your creativity, and jump into altered states of consciousness.

UNITED STATES
P U B L I S H I N G

AVAILABLE THROUGH: S.E.E. PUBLISHING

The Hathors' Self-Mastery Exercises
on Audio Tape

The Self-Mastery Exercises in The Hathor Material book are also available on a convenient audio cassette tape. The tape was recorded by channel Tom Kenyon.

On this tape, Tom uses his remarkable four-octave vocal range, accompanied by the Tibetan bowl, to call the names of the archangels. This extraordinary sound called "toning" lifts one's subtle bodies into a high frequency state as a prelude to doing one or more of the Self-Mastery Exercises.

Tom guides the listener through each exercise and incorporates background psychoacoustic sound tracks to facilitate integration of the exercises. A special heart-opening meditation with the Hathors is also included!

Single cassette T102 $9.95.

Tom Kenyon's ABR Audio Products

In 1983 Tom Kenyon, M.A., formed Acoustic Brain Research (ABR) to scientifically document the effects of sound and music on human consciousness. As a psychological counselor and musician, Tom discovered that sound and music could be powerful catalysts for both personal growth and healing. By enrolling the efforts of numerous researchers in both private and university settings, ABR has substantially documented the positive benefits of psychoacoustic technology.

Since November 1997, S.E.E. Publishing Company has been distributing all of Tom's ABR tapes and compact discs. S.E.E. also sells Tom's book Brain States.

ABR tapes are remarkably successful in helping you achieve the self-enrichment and self-empowerment goals you seek. This is because of the scientific research, creative artistry, and advanced technology ABR invests in each program.

Music and sound have, from man's earliest cultures, been known to influence our states of mind. Now, through the application of advanced engineering, ABR utilizes the physics and psychology of sound to bring new scientific meaning and direction to this wondrous phenomenon.

ABR technology uses a variety of natural and electronic sounds, including specific sound patterns and frequencies,

 Spiritual Education Endeavors Publishing Company
1556 Halford Avenue #288, Santa Clara, CA 95051-2661
USA (408) 245-5457

differentiations of tone and vibration, synchronization, oscillations and pulsations, verbal and non-verbal input, tonal architecture, and hemispheric spanning. These are all orchestrated to stimulate the brain/mind into more resourceful states of awareness. Today, ABR is a recognized leader in psychoacoustic development and is acknowledged by professionals and lay persons alike as a source of the most advanced and neurologically-sound audio tapes available today.

BioPulse Technology™

ABR psychoacoustic technology is based on the use of complex tonal matrices in which various sound patterns are mixed to stimulate the brain/mind into more resourceful states. Many of these tones are mixed beneath the level of audible hearing, masked by other sounds, or sometimes music, specifically composed for the desired mental/emotional state.

ABR tapes and CD's also take advantage of "biopulse technology™" in which specific tones, known to affect brain states, are mixed into the tonal matrix. Research indicates that such frequencies can significantly alter awareness. These biopulse frequencies fall into a few broad categories, and a parenthetical note after each tape title/description indicates which biopulse frequencies are used.

The primary categories of the biopulse frequencies are:

Delta (0.5-4 Hz) - associated with deep levels of relaxation such as sleep

Theta (4-8 Hz) - associated with tranquil states of awareness in which vivid internal imagery often occurs

Alpha (8-12 Hz) - relaxed nervous system, ideal for stress management, accelerated learning, and mental imagery

Beta (12-30 Hz) - associated with waking/alert states of awareness

K-Complex (30-35 Hz) - clarity and sudden states of integration, the "ah-ha" experience

Super High Beta (35-150 Hz) - psychodynamic states of awareness

 Spiritual Education Endeavors Publishing Company
1556 Halford Avenue #288, Santa Clara, CA 95051-2661
USA (408) 245-5457

AUDIO PRODUCT DESCRIPTIONS

Relaxation and Stress Management

Sound Bath
Soothe and relax yourself with this wonderful mix of beautiful music and ambient nature sounds. One of our most popular tapes for relaxation. (Theta range)
Single cassette T209 $13.95, compact disc CD209 $16.95

Wave Form
Wave Form gently "massages" your brain, helping you to dissolve tensions and drift into deeply relaxing states of awareness. (Theta range)
Single cassette T202 $13.95 *Headphones suggested.*

Wave Form II
Based on an ancient mantra believed to be the sound of the inner heart, this tonal matrix gently "opens the heart" thereby raising consciousness to a purer state of awareness, self-awareness and harmony. Beautiful vocals are intertwined with deep harmonic musical passages. (Theta range)
Single cassette T207 $13.95 *Headphones suggested.*

Rest and Relaxation (R & R)
For busy people who don't always get the rest they need, this tape includes *The 24-Minute Nap* and *The 22-Minute Vacation.* People love this tape! (Mid-Alpha to low Delta range)
Single cassette T402 $13.95 *Headphones suggested.*

Homage to Sol
Beautiful repetitive tempos for guitar, flute, and cello. Based on discoveries of the Lozamov Institute, this beautiful and restful music opens new vistas of serenity.
Single cassette T201 $13.95

Meditation

The Ghandarva Experience
A powerful journey into the spiritual realms of being. This unique program includes a 30-minute talk on the history of the Ghandarva and traces its roots back to Vedic India. Part Two is a compelling listening experience and includes the Chant of the Archangels and the Calling of Sacred Names, the Ghandarvic Choir, and a beautiful rendition of the 23rd Psalm.
Single cassette T801 $13.95, compact disc CD801 $16.95

Singing Crystal Bowls

Ethereal sounds of quartz "singing crystal bowls" to enhance altered states of awareness. Stimulate your body's energy centers as the "crystal vibrations" flow throughout your body.
Single cassette T203 $13.95

New Video Tape Available

Sound Healing and the Inner Terrain of Consciousness. Tom explores the New Physics and its applications to Sound Healing. Part Two, **Song of the New Earth**, is a video collage of natural scenes from around the world. This visual experience has been mixed with a stereo sound-track of Tom's healing sounds. Approximately 60 minutes.
Video cassette(VCR)V101 $29.95

Fitness

The Zone

A delightful and truly effective tape designed to be used with a "Walkman-type" cassette player while doing aerobic exercises such as running, walking, etc. Increases your self motivation and encourages a more intense workout. (Alpha-Beta)
Single cassette tape T605 $13.95 *Headphones suggested.*

Self-Healing and Recovery

Psycho-Immunology

This widely acclaimed "self-healing" program helps you to explore the body/mind connection. It has been created to help you develop a greater potential for "healing experiences," and to assist you in your natural self-healing abilities. Note: Not a substitute for medical treatment. (Alpha-Delta)
Set of 3 tapes T401 $49.95 *Headphones suggested.*

Yoga for the Eyes

This tape offers eye movement exercises, guided imagery, and musical patterns to help rejuvenate your physically-strained and stress-weary sight. (Mid-Alpha range)
Single cassette tape T608 $13.95 *Stereo headphones required.*

Freedom To Be

Free yourself to make healthier decisions and live a fuller life. Designed as a recovery program for alcoholism and drug addiction, these tapes have been found to be very helpful with

issues of low self-esteem, self-sabotage, and emotional overwhelm. (Theta) *Headphones suggested.*
Two tape set with instructions T602 $29.95

Transformation Now!
A highly intense psychoacoustic stimulation of the brain/mind for rapid personal transformation. Note: Epileptics and persons with brain damage should not listen to this tape without professional help. (Shifts rapidly thru Alpha, Theta, and Delta)
Single cassette tape T302 $13.95 *Headphones suggested.*

Healing the Child Within
Unique guided imagery helps you to resolve deeply-held childhood issues. (Alpha to Theta range)
Single cassette tape T601 $13.95 *Headphones suggested.*

Mind/Brain Performance Increase
Creative Imaging
Processes used with this tape have been documented in independent tests to significantly improve analytical abilities, creative problem solving, learning, and insight. Protocols accompanying the tape can also be used to increase visualization abilities. (Mid-Alpha)
Single cassette T205 $13.95 *Headphones suggested.*

Mind Gymnastiks
This "flagship" of ABR's programs has been hailed by researchers, professionals, and laypersons as a highly innovative and powerful tool for helping to increase mental abilities and performance. Users report expanded creativity, speed of processing, perceptual clarity, and feelings of "being on top." (Low Delta to K-complex) *Stereo headphones required.*
Set of 6 tapes with instructions T700 $99.95

Inspired: High Genius and Creativity
Utilizing visual imagery and sophisticated archetypal psychology, these participatory tapes help you tap into the creative principles that great scientists and artists have used throughout history. Enter meditative states where enhanced visualization and inspired dreams help you gain insights into problem solving and goal attainment. (Mid-Alpha range) *Headphones suggested.*
Set of 4 cassette tapes with manual T701 $89.95

The Spiritual Unfoldment Network (S.U.N.) was founded by Irving Feurst. It is an international, non-denominational, spiritually-oriented network of teachers dedicated to making available to the public esoteric energy work from all major spiritual traditions. Our goal is to assist people in progressing more effectively on their personal spiritual path, at their own pace, without prescribing what that path must be.

All S.U.N. classes are *initiation* workshops in which you receive powerful energies that you can then access at any time for yourself or others by mentally directing the flow (no visualization or complex symbols required). The versatility and ease of use of S.U.N. energies make them perfect for even the complete beginner, yet their power and sophistication surprises even most professional energy workers.

Dozens of different classes are taught by S.U.N. teachers, including ones on Hawaiian and Tibetan energies, chakras, angels, mantras, kundalini, connecting to your Higher Self and much, much more. **All S.U.N. Teachers can teach a special course "Enhancing Energy Blessings from the Stars", which significantly strengthens all the initiations in this book.** The frequencies used in this class are such that you <u>must</u> take it in person and you <u>must</u> first have received all the initiations in this book.

For more information about S.U.N. classes, either visit our web site at **www.spiritunfold.com** or write: S.U.N., c/o Irving Feurst (see "How To Receive Information" section). S.U.N. classes are taken in person. If there is not already a S.U.N. teacher in your area, some teachers are willing to travel if enough students are interested. In addition to teaching classes, a number of S.U.N. teachers do private sessions which draw on the many different S.U.N. energies.

Khu, The Egyptian Mystery School ™

Khu (a word referring to the higher levels of the soul) was founded by Irving Feurst and passes on ancient Egyptian soul teachings and energy initiations in their original and pure form. The school specifically de-emphasizes ritual and makes no effort to contact the Egyptian spiritual guides (which some refer to as "gods" and "goddesses.") The work of the school centers around personality-soul fusion. Through extensive initiations, students are empowered to form "soul vehicles" which are projected to temples on other planets. Here they receive energy initiations for personality-soul fusion from masters in these temples.

The Khu school also studies ancient Egyptian insights into the hidden nature of manifestation and techniques for implementing these insights, Egyptian alchemical practices for transforming the elements in the subtle bodies, and Egyptian tantric practices for accelerating spiritual evolution and heightening sexual pleasure.

Khu has a narrower focus than S.U.N., since it uses only ancient Egyptian energies. Unlike S.U.N. classes, Khu classes are not taken in person. They are taught through a combination of written lessons and distant initiation. A requirement for participating in the school is to sign and return a "Solar Angel Contract" which you will receive as part of your information packet (a sample contract is in the book). For more information on Khu visit the school's web site at **www.egyptianmysteryschool.com** or write: Khu, c/o Irving Feurst (see "How To Receive Information" section below).

—— HOW TO RECEIVE INFORMATION ——

If you have Internet access, please check our web sites for the most up-to-date information on S.U.N. and Khu. If not, please write to the address below. *Do not* call or write the *publisher* of this book; they will just refer you to this page. Please know that Irving has been guided to help humanity through teaching classes and does not do private sessions, consultations or readings of any sort. He does not give personal or medical advice and does not do healing. If you have a medical condition, please consult a licensed health practitioner.

ADDRESS: Specify "S.U.N." or "Khu" on the first address line, c/o Irving Feurst, 4100-10 Redwood Rd. #370, Oakland, CA 94619.

LOVE CORPS NETWORKING

The term *Love Corps* was coined in the book *New Teachings for an Awakening Humanity*. The Love Corps is a universal alliance of all human beings of good will who seek both inner personal peace and its planetary application. Thus the world-wide Love Corps family is committed to achieving inner peace through meditation and self-healing and to sharing that peace in groups where the unity of cooperation can be applied toward the preservation of all life.

In order to support our light-workers, wherever they may be, we publish the Love Corps Newsletter. Its purpose is to keep our Love Corps family informed of the very latest information being received from the Spiritual Hierarchy. Newsletter subscribers are eligible to join the Love Corps Network. Please send a SASE for an application.

Virginia Essene frequently travels around the United States and the world to link Love Corps energies, to share additional information not included in the books—*Energy Blessings from the Stars; The Hathor Material: Messages from an Ascended Civilization; You Are Becoming a Galactic Human; New Cells, New Bodies, New Life!; New Teachings for an Awakening Humanity;* and three other out-of-print titles—and to encourage humanity's achievement of peace and the preservation of all life upon planet earth.

Please contact us for further information if you would like to be involved in the Love Corps endeavors or to participate with us in seminars. Contact us to schedule a soul reading or an individual counseling session, in person or by telephone.

This "Time of Awakening" brings a new spiral of information to move each of us to a higher level of inner peace and planetary involvement. You are encouraged to accept the responsibility of this evolutionary opportunity and immediately unite efforts with other people in creating peaceful attitudes and conditions on our planet.

SHARE FOUNDATION
1556 Halford Ave. #288
Santa Clara, CA 95051-2661 USA
Tel. (408) 245-5457   FAX (408) 245-5460
E-mail: lovecorp@ix.netcom.com

ORDER FORM - part 1 of 2

Audio & Video Items (T = tape, CD = comp. disc, V = video)

Title	Code	Price	Qty	Title	Code	Price	Qty
Creative Imag.	T205	$13.95	____	Rest & Relax.	T402	$13.95	____
Freedom to Be	T602	$29.95	____	Singing C.B.	T203	$13.95	____
Ghandarva E.	T801	$13.95	____	Sound Bath	T209	$13.95	____
Healing . . .	T601	$13.95	____	The Zone	T605	$13.95	____
Homage to S.	T201	$13.95	____	Trans. Now!	T302	$13.95	____
Inspired: . . .	T701	$89.95	____	Wave Form	T202	$13.95	____
Mind Gymn.	T700	$99.95	____	Wave Form II	T207	$13.95	____
Psycho-Imm.	T401	$49.95	____	Yoga . . . Eyes	T608	$13.95	____

Transform Your Cellular Water Field .... T103 $12.95 ____

Hathors' Self-Mastery Exercises tape .... T102 $ 9.95 ____

Ghandarva Experience .... CD801 $16.95 ____

Sound Bath .... CD209 $16.95 ____

Sound Healing in the Inner Terrain of
Consciousness with Tom Kenyon, video .... V101 $29.95 ____

Total of audio tapes, CD's, and videos (U.S. $) $_____ •

Books

Energy Blessings from the Stars ....@ $14.95 $_____ •

The Hathor Material ....@ $12.95 $_____ •

New Cells, New Bodies, NEW LIFE! ....@ $11.95 $_____ •

New Teachings for an Awakening Humanity:
    English ed. **(Revised 1994/1995)** ....@ $9.95 $_____ •
    Spanish ed. **Nuevas Ensenanzas** ....@ $9.95 $_____ •
       or (Spanish only) 2 books for $10.00 ....$_____ •

Brain States by Tom Kenyon ....@ $11.95 $_____ •

Minus quantity discount (books only, see next page) .... $(_____) •

        Product total (above items marked •) $_____

Plus 8.25% **sales tax** (California residents only) .... $_____

Plus **shipping & handling** (see next page): .... $_____
    (Amount is based on **Product total**, above)

Please send me the **Love Corps Newsletter**:
    One year (bi-monthly) subscription = $24 .... $_____
    Canadian & other international = $30 (airmail) .... $_____
    Earlier issues @ $4/issue U.S.A., $5 foreign. Specify
    year & mo. _____ J/F, M/A, M/J, J/A, S/O, N/D .. $_____

Love Corps donation (tax deductible, see next page) .... $_____

TOTAL ENCLOSED (add items within box) .... $_____

NOTE: Be sure to complete part 2 of the order form >>>>>>>>>

ORDER FORM - part 2 of 2

To: **S.E.E. PUBLISHING COMPANY**
c/o The SHARE FOUNDATION*
1556 Halford Avenue #288
Santa Clara, CA 95051-2661 U.S.A.
Telephone (408) 245-5457   FAX (408) 245-5460
E-mail: lovecorp@ix.netcom.com (for info only)

Quantity discounts; books only:
  5 to 9 books - take off 10%
  10 or more books - take off 20%

U.S. Shipping & Handling Charges

Product total $	Amount	Product total $	Amount
$00.00 - $14.99	$3.95	$45.00 - $59.99	$8.45
$15.00 - $29.99	$5.45	$60.00 - $74.99	$9.95
$30.00 - $44.99	$6.95	$75.00 - $99.99	$11.45
		$100.00 and up	$12.95

Notes:

• Canada & Mexico add $2.00 to above Shipping amounts.

• Other International charges vary by country and weight; please call, FAX, or e-mail for rates.

• Please send check or money order in **U.S. funds** payable through a U.S. bank, or send an International money order made payable to S.E.E. Publishing Co. We **do not accept** foreign currency, or checks drawn on a foreign bank.

• We will ship your order by the best carrier. Some carriers do not deliver to P.O. boxes, so we must have both your street and postal address. Please request shipping rates for first class or air mail.

• All prices and shipping & handling charges are subject to change.

• The Share Foundation is a non-profit organization. Contributions are tax deductible under section 501(c)(3) of the IRS code.

Please PRINT (this information is for your mailing label)

_____
Name

_____
Address

_____
City   State/Province   Zip Code
(_____)_____
Area Code   Telephone Number (optional)

NOTES

NOTES